BEHIND THE
SHADES

A Female Secret Service Agent's
True Story

SUE ANN BAKER

I have tried to recreate events, locales, and conversations from my memories of them. In order to maintain their anonymity, in some instances I have changed the names of individuals and places, as well as some identifying characteristics.

Published by WWP Publishing
444 NE Winchester St.
Roseburg, OR 97471
www.sueannbaker.com

ISBN: 978-0-9961595-1-7 (E-Book)
ISBN: 978-0-9961595-0-0 (Softcover)
ISBN: 978-0-9961595-2-4 (Hardcover)

Library of Congress Control Number: 2015905461

Cover design by Heidi Gress

Manufactured in the United States of America

First Edition 2015

Dedication

To my brother, Jim, whose infinite patience taught my stubby child's fingers to properly type on our vintage Underwood typewriter, and later to waltz on his shoes. To my parents, who unknowingly nurtured their alpha daughter and gave me enough confidence to grab unexpected opportunities. To my nieces, nephews, family, and friends, who always wanted to hear my stories and urged me to leave this legacy.

I love you all.

"He who refuses to embrace a unique opportunity loses the prize as surely as if he failed."

William James

Table of Contents

Part III 1972 Presidential Campaign

Part IV Los Angeles

Epilogue

Recipes

Biography

Foreword

The United States Secret Service, established on July 5, 1865, had been, from its inception, a male-only law-enforcement agency. It wasn't until 1970 that, slowly, that began to change. It became apparent that having females in the Secret Service was necessary to carry out the agency mission. The question was: how do we go about obtaining quality personnel, and then how do we best use them?

At the time, I was Deputy Assistant Director of Protective Forces and was involved in the decision-making process. I personally knew how valuable these female employees could be in protective assignments. I had been responsible for the protection and safety of Mrs. Jacqueline Kennedy from November 1960 to November 1964, and during that time wished many times that a female Secret Service agent had been there with me. It would have eliminated many embarrassing situations and added immensely to the protective effort being provided.

We decided to seek out candidates that were highly motivated and had skills that could transfer into the organizational needs. We began with seven female recruits and placed them in the Uniformed Division called the Executive Protective Service (EPS). The women were not uniformed, and initially, the training they received was mostly "on the job."

Sue Ann Baker was one of these seven women selected for the first-ever, female enforcement positions within the US Secret Service. Although each of these seven young women initially carried the title Officer, EPS, on December 15, 1971, five of the seven were sworn in as Agents, United States Secret Service. It was a proud day for these women, and an historic day for the organization. We were finally catching up to the needs and reality of the times.

Although I was a member of the headquarters staff when the decision was made to admit females into the agent corps of the US Secret Service, I must admit that I didn't fully realize the challenges these women faced.

Behind the Shades tells the story of the life of a female agent entering the male-dominated world of the Secret Service. It is a story of personal sacrifice, adventure, acceptance and rejection, tenacity, endurance, and hard work during trying times. Sue Ann Baker was on the front lines of history and observed it being made on a larger scale. She is one of the pioneers who paved the way for the many capable female agents that followed in her footsteps, and I am proud to say I served with her.

Clinton J. Hill
Assistant Director, Protective Forces (Retired)
United States Secret Service

Acknowledgements

People told me for years that I should write a book about my life, and particularly about my life in the US Secret Service. The years have had a way of flying by, however, and the overwhelming task of writing a book was always put on the back burner. When I retired in 2014, after twenty-one years as a financial planner, I had no excuses, only my fear to overcome.

I want to thank Lisa McCubbin and Clint Hill for their support and encouragement early on when I hit the key and sent them an email that their book, *Mrs. Kennedy and Me*, inspired me to record my part in history. With that email, I felt I was committed. Next I informed my family and friends, who obviously were excited about the prospect of reading the finished product. As I experienced the emotional ups and downs of writing, they were always there with a sympathetic ear, a two-mile walk, or a glass of wine. I apologize for any lengthy whining I may have bored them with.

A heartfelt thanks goes to Michael Sampson, archivist for the US Secret Service. He was a wealth of knowledge, incredibly helpful in finding background information, and a joy to work with. Reminiscing with Jerry Parr, Glen Winn, Denise Ferrenz, Phyllis Shantz, Holly (Hufschmidt) Van Fleet, Jeanne Doyle, and Maurice Butler helped bring back memories I'd forgotten. Other memories were revived when Agent Hazel Cerra found all of the *first five* and brought us back together again in 2007 at Secret Service Headquarters for Women's History Month. She was amazed we were all still alive! It was then that I realized we were old enough to *be* history. New acquaintances I made among female agents in today's Secret Service, and also during a Women in Federal Law Enforcement conference, gave me a perspective on how far women have come, but also how far they have to go to truly enjoy respect and equality. I thank all of them for their time and their tales. For the photo collection, thanks goes to the *NY Daily News*, the Associated Press, the Nixon Library, the Secret Service, and to my mother for keeping my personal photos.

For their professionalism, knowledge, hand-holding, and advice, I want to thank my editor, Lindsey Alexander, for making my first attempt at writing better than I could have imagined; Deana Riddle, my book interior designer for pulling everything together and making it look professional; Mary Giuseffi, my image consultant for making me look better; Heidi Gress, my book cover designer and photographer, who knows how to use a soft lens; and Steve Harrison of Bradley Communications for his ongoing encouragement and access to his wonderful staff of publicity and marketing consultants. It seems it does take a village to raise an author.

Part I:

Executive Protective Service: Washington, DC

Chapter 1:

July 1971 The Princess is Lost – Am I to Blame?

As I drove into Camp Oneka, a picturesque retreat in Pennsylvania's Poconos Mountains, the smell of freshly mown grass and morning air did little to calm my nerves. My excitement had turned to apprehension about five miles out. Now, as I parked beneath an ancient maple tree near the camp office, fear of failure loomed in my mind. What if my limited training wasn't enough? What if *I* wasn't enough?

Summoning what self-confidence I could, I took a deep breath and stepped out of my little yellow Volkswagen bug and into my first assignment. *I can do this*, I thought. *I can do this.*

For the past hundred summers, Camp Oneka had welcomed girls from well-heeled Philadelphia families. On July 23, 1971, fourteen-year-old Princess Caroline Grimaldi of Monaco became one of those girls. Her mother, American movie star Grace Kelly, had spent summers at Camp Oneka in her youth and now wanted her daughter to carry on a tradition. Committed to giving their daughter a "normal" camping experience, Princess Grace and Prince Rainier had declined federal protection for her. And so, unbeknownst to Princess Caroline or her parents, I'd been charged with Caroline's protection, working undercover for the Secret Service.

My cover? Camp counselor.

My first order of business was to meet with Henrietta Deubler and her sister, Emily, the co-owners of Camp Oneka. Swallowing my nerves, I knocked on the door of their large log home. The door edged opened and one of the sisters appeared. "Yes, may I help you?"

"Hi, are you Miss Deubler?"

"I am," replied Henrietta, the taller of the two sisters. They looked alike and both wore outdated hairstyles of relatively short, tightly curled brown hair that still showed bobby pin marks.

"Hello, I'm Sue Ann Baker. I've been assigned to protect Princess Caroline."

"Yes, we've been expecting you. Come on in." As I entered the room, a sickly sweet odor of cheap lavender perfume and moldiness hit me in the face. My eyes quickly swept the room. The faded floral couch and easy chair kept company with a rustic coffee table supported by two massive tree stumps.

Inviting me to sit at a small rough-hewn oak dining table, Emily offered me a glass of her homemade lemonade. My thirst gauge was on zero after my five-hour drive from DC.

"Yes, please, that would be great." I smiled.

We talked about what I could expect during the next three weeks. Henrietta, the sterner-looking of the two, took the lead.

"Despite what you may have been told, Ms. Baker, Caroline's counselor has already been assigned. But don't worry: your tent won't be too far from her."

Too far? Too far for what? Too far to hear Caroline scream? Too far to stop an abduction?

Though the Deubler sisters seemed somewhat relieved that I was there to help take some of the responsibility of safeguarding royalty off their shoulders, they seemed less than sure as to how I would fit in. They also let me know, right off the bat, that no matter what instructions I'd been given by my supervisors, the camp was their domain, and they operated it as they saw fit. Fine! I guess I could hear her scream if a kidnapper tried to abduct her. But what if he covered her face with a chloroform-drenched rag? Given my previous Washington, DC, police training, I couldn't help but think like a criminal. Slamming that frightening door shut in my mind, I tried to focus on the woman in front of me. Henrietta was waiting for my reaction. I conscientiously put on the poker face I'd been cultivating—every agent had one.

"And by the way," Henrietta continued, "you'll need

to leave your gun with Mrs. McGlinn, the camp nurse. Her cabin is only about fifty yards from the tent you will be living in. We can't take the chance of one of the girls finding it."

A worst-case scenario flashed through my mind: A kidnapper grabbing Caroline and pulling her from her bed, Caroline trying to fight him off, the other girls screaming, and me flying out of my tent . . . gunless. Could this get any worse?

"So, Sue Ann, what can you do?" she asked. I was puzzled. I didn't think she meant shooting guns or jumping on and off the running boards of moving cars.

"What do you mean, 'What can I do'?"

"This is camp, Sue Ann, not reform school. The girls play sports, they go sailing, they like swimming and water skiing, they do crafts and put on plays. You have to teach *something*."

"I can swim," I offered hesitantly.

Henrietta sighed. "That's it?"

"I've water skied."

"Great," Henrietta said swiftly, making a note on her planner, "you'll teach swimming to the younger girls and water skiing to the teenagers."

My startled silence must have alarmed her, because, snapping her planner closed, she said, "You have taken at least a water safety course, have you not?"

I had not.

Emily, the quieter of the Deubler sisters, gently pushed a copy of the *Red Cross Book on Swimming and Water Safety* across the table to me. "This might be helpful," she said with a sly grin. I thanked her and stuffed it

4

in my purse.

Before showing me to the cabin I'd be sharing for the first night with Caroline, the Deublers reviewed my cover story with me. As we walked down a soft, pine-needled path past fading pink rhododendrons toward the lake, they introduced me to other counselors as a graduate student. Although I was older than the other counselors, I looked younger than my twenty-five years.

When Caroline Grimaldi and her cousin arrived later that day, I tried not to stare at her. For one thing, she was darkly beautiful with long, silky brown hair and high cheekbones. At fourteen, she favored her mother. Even if I hadn't known she was a princess, I would have known she came from wealth.

Henrietta introduced me to Caroline's aunt and Prince Rainier III. He and Grace Kelly had met in Monaco in April 1955. After corresponding privately for several months, the prince came to America that December and reportedly proposed to her after only three days. Dubbed "the wedding of the century," their nuptials were aired on TV and watched by millions. That year, I'd spent hours playing with my Princess Grace and Prince Rainier paper dolls, carefully cutting out Grace Kelly's gorgeous wedding dress.

Now, in Prince Rainier's presence, I felt ten years old again. I was meeting a real prince. My heart pounded in my chest. He was shorter than I imagined with thundercloud-gray hair. He seemed shy, perhaps because he was out of his element. The lush, tree-studded countryside of rural Pennsylvania must have been quite a change from his palace in Monaco.

Tamping down butterflies, I managed to say, "How do you do, Your Highness? It's a pleasure to meet you."

With a slight bow of his head, he answered with a rich French accent, "My pleasure. I hope you have a wonderful time here at camp with Caroline." After giving his daughter a quick hug, he climbed back into his chauffeured black Caddy and sped away.

The next day, we moved into our separate tents. Set on wooden platforms, they were sparsely furnished with single metal beds. The mattresses were so thin you could practically see through them. Our metal trunks fit snugly under the beds, and my campers and I each had a small wooden nightstand. That night, after I got the girls quieted down and asleep, I pulled the covers over my head, turned on my flashlight, and read the *Red Cross Manual*. Undercover agent indeed.

Lakeside tent section at Camp Oneka.

I spent the next few days settling in. I'd forgotten so much from my Girl Scout camping days: the lingo, the songs, the bells, the gongs, and the bugles. At first, I felt inadequate. I had experience in many things, but I didn't think I did any of them well. My curiosity and wide variety of interests had given me a broad view of the world, but I never had any interest in spending all my time becoming proficient in just one thing—that would have been boring. I did my best to assimilate into a culture and setting with which I was totally unfamiliar.

Fortunately, two counselors recognized my bewilderment and showed me the ropes. After the first week, they invited me to join them and some other counselors on a late-night excursion. The plan was to sneak across the road into the woods after the kids were asleep. First, we needed provisions. Cheese and crackers filched from the camp kitchen appeared, and someone had procured a couple of bottles of wine. Smoking and chatting, we bonded over boys, hair, makeup, boys, campers, the stingy Deubler sisters, and boys. On this and other counselor forays, I always drank Coke, in case something happened to Caroline and I needed my wits about me. Sometimes, instead of wandering into the woods, we only went to the far end of the tennis court. I felt much more at ease sticking close to camp, and as the days went by, I had to invent a reason why I didn't want to go roaming around the Poconos at midnight.

My invention was a boyfriend, "Bob."

Bob was staying in a cabin on the other side of the lake for the summer. He also was in graduate school, and we'd been dating for a year and a half. Bob satisfied not only the counselors' questions, but also my four-teen-year-old campers' questions. "How old were you when you first kissed a boy? Do you have a lot of boy-friends? How did you meet him? How old is he? How old are you? Are you going to marry him? Is he handsome?" OK, Sue Ann, get the lying side of your brain in gear.

Bob also gave me an excuse to get out of camp once a week. In fact, Bob was my detail leader Geoffrey, a se-nior agent who had the cushy (and boring) job of sitting in a hotel room approximately twelve miles from the camp. Believe it or not, Geoffrey was my backup.

Because there were no cell phones in those days, if I wanted to reach him, I had to sneak into the nurse's cabin and use her phone. We'd arrange a time to meet in town. I'm not sure who saved whose sanity. He was stuck watching TV, reading, eating, and sleeping. I was stuck with few adults to talk to, and no stimulating con-versation. Over a quiet drink, I'd bring him up to date on Caroline's activities, and he'd bring me up to date on what was going on in the world outside of Camp Oneka.

Two weeks into my assignment, I learned we'd be taking an overnight canoe trip with the older girls. I wanted to make sure I was covered. After discussing the logistics of how he would support me on the lake, I re-luctantly left the air-conditioned motel room, stepped into the hot, humid, buggy summer afternoon, and drove slowly back to my cloistered reality.

On the day of the overnight trip, we hoisted our ca-noes over our heads and marched to the lake. On the first day, we paddled our canoes for two hours to get to the campsite. When we arrived, I was exhausted.

My shoulders ached, and I realized how out of shape I was. Smoking didn't help. Worse yet, in the distance, my backup was lounging in a *motorboat*. No paddling for him, and with his .357 Magnum, he probably felt less naked than I did. As for my gun, it was still safely hiding back in Nurse McGlinn's office.

Unloading canoes for overnight trip at Camp Oneka. Princess Caroline at far left.

That afternoon, we goofed off with the canoes—sinking them and then climbing on them. When we finally reached the Oneka cabin, the girls cooked hotdogs over a wood fire until the sun went down and storm clouds rolled in. A soft rain started falling at ten, and everyone moved into the cabin for the night. There was one rickety table in the corner near a fireplace, but not much else.

Except bats.

All night long, bats swooped down from the ceiling and flew around the room, terrifying the girls. The discomfort of sleeping on the hard wooden floor was compounded by their shrieks and petrified giggles. Nobody slept much. As I lay there looking up at the cabin's beams and listening to the sound of tiny wings flapping overhead, I wondered what I'd gotten myself into. This was a far cry from the environment I'd expected to be working in—the White House.

I hadn't trained for this. Hell, I hadn't even been sworn in. Instead, along with six other female officers, I was being tested as a US Secret Service Agent. We were all being tested. The Secret Service had never hired women agents before. This was completely new territory—for them and for us. The stakes of success suddenly seemed immensely heavy. If Princess Caroline were bitten by a rabid bat, if she fell out of her canoe and hit her head, if a backwoods bad guy abducted her in the middle of the night, my failure to protect her would scuttle my chance to be a Secret Service Agent. But would my failure scuttle this chance for other women, too?

By the next morning, the rain had stopped. The sun warmed us as we scrambled eggs over a wood fire. We rolled up our sleeping bags, climbed into our canoes, and paddled another two hours to the end of the lake. We pulled our canoes up on shore near the mouth of a river that flowed into the lake and ate lunch. After waiting for our lunch to settle, the girls decided it would be fun to dive off a twenty-five-foot-high bridge into the lake. I put on my invisible lifeguard hat, took pictures, and tried to control my fears of what *might* happen. The what ifs sped around my brain with the speed of an atom smasher. A few hours later, my worst fear came to pass, and this time I wasn't imagining it.

Campers jumping from bridge on the overnight canoe
trip at Camp Oneka.

We started to paddle our canoes back to Camp Oneka.
The counselors knew where there was one last oppor-

tunity to land our canoes, eat a spaghetti dinner, and take a short hike. After dinner, we led the group, single file, up a beautiful, icy-cold, spring-fed creek. We had hiked a half mile into the woods when we turned around and headed back toward our canoes. The girls had a great time splashing each other with the cold water. One girl shrieked when she slipped on a moss-covered rock and almost fell. I turned around to see if she was OK and to check for Caroline and her cousin. They were gone! Cold water swirled around my feet. Beads of sweat rolled down my forehead. The counselors were concerned, but I nearly panicked. I'd lost her! Could someone lurking in the woods have grabbed the girls? Everyone started backtracking, looking for them in earnest. We called and called their names as the minutes slowly crept by. Part of my brain was composing my report—and resignation—to my superiors, and the other part was in meltdown mode.

Finally, Caroline and her cousin came running out of the brush. With a toss of her head, Caroline laughed. "Here we are. What kept you so long? We've been waiting." They thought it was great fun to hide and watch us look for them. I was torn between relief and wanting to strangle her.

At the end of three weeks, the camp was a flurry of activity as campers stripped their beds, packed their trunks, swept out the tent floor, and excitedly waited for their parents to arrive. I was excited to get home myself. Princess Caroline was going back to her lavish lifestyle unharmed. Decidedly, I'd passed the test. I felt pretty good about it, since I'd had to make up the rules as I went along. How many more tests would there be, I wondered. And would I fail one?

As my colleague, Kathy, always said, "Sometimes you just have to play it by ear, even if you don't know the tune."

Camp Oneka. I'm in the top row, and Caroline is in the third row down.

Chapter 2:

May 1945: The Manhattan Project—My Secret City

Twenty-two days after Hitler committed suicide in a Berlin bunker, and fifteen days after Germany surrendered in World War II, my father, Morell Baker, huddled in the backseat of his 1941 Chevy over his eight-year-old daughter Carol, cradling her crushed head in his lap. The car sped toward the hospital, weaving through the empty streets. My mother, Ruth, ran two red lights, arriving at the hospital emergency entrance in seven minutes flat. But Morell knew it didn't matter. By the time he stepped out of the car to hand Carol to the paramedics, blood had pooled in the crotch of his gabardine pants.

The child's limp body was quickly placed on the gurney and wheeled inside.

Though I wasn't born yet, the family story is etched in my mind like fine Waterford crystal. My parents had decided to see a movie. Carol and her ten-year-old brother, Jimmie, begged and begged to go. So much for date night, my mother thought.

"OK, go get cleaned up," she told them. "We'll leave in twenty minutes for the show."

Carol pleaded to play on the swing set while my parents got ready.

"That's fine, Carol, but don't get your dress dirty. Jimmie, you need to change your pants."

Carol, the brown-haired girl who loved beautiful things, ran out to the swing set near the house and stood on the seat, wrapping her small hands around the ropes, leaning back and pumping—flying higher and higher. Soon, a neighbor girl joined her. From inside, Ruth heard them laughing. She combed her hair and gathered her handbag, glad to hear her daughter so happy. But at six forty-five, a piercing wail sliced open the blue sky.

Rummaging through my brother's attic sixty-six years later, I found the letter my mother had written to her mother on the day of my sister's burial. My hands trembled as I opened it. I had never seen it before. In her beautiful penmanship, my mother wrote:

The swing she was on was built on a frame, but not fastened to the ground. The whole thing fell over and the 4x4 that held the ropes struck Carol's forehead and killed her instantly. How I wish you could be here today and see our baby. She is so beautiful, lying there in that little white casket, with a blue dress on, and her long braids hanging over each shoulder with a blue ribbon on each one and pink sweet peas in her hand from Jimmie.

That swing set, situated on a hillside by the Army Corps of Engineers, had toppled over as if flicked by the fingers of God. The same God Morell refused to acknowledge for years after that day, sure that if there were a God, he would not have taken his child's life.

Swing set that killed my sister.

Another box in my brother's attic contained my grandmother's Bible, in which she'd written the date of Carol's death. I did the math, shocked to realize that my parents conceived me a mere four months after Carol's death. Often, couples experiencing the death of a child get divorced. Before Carol's death, my parents had had the perfect family—two children, a boy and a girl, with a comfortable two years between them. My mother had fought high blood pressure for years. I'm sure she never intended to get pregnant again, but Carol's death changed that. My mother's decision made her Catholic doctor so nervous he threatened to abort me if her blood pressure went over two hundred. To everyone's relief, I arrived safely on June 27, 1946. I grew up aware that I was not an accident, aware that I was wanted, and feeling destined for great things. I firmly believe I would not exist had my sister not died. The feeling of responsibility for making my life count still lurks in the hidden folds of my brain.

1945 - Jimmie, Ruth, Morell, and Carol Baker.

I was born in the so-called "secret city" of Oak Ridge, Tennessee, about twenty-five miles west of Knoxville. The city was so secret, it wasn't even on the maps. Oak Ridge had been established in 1942 as the production site for the Manhattan Project, the international effort to develop the atomic bomb. Originally called the Clinton Engineering Works, houses had been seized by the US government and the local population evicted. Temporary prefab housing sprung up. My family lived in a color-coded yellow 550-square-foot box. To cool the house in the hot summertime, my father ingeniously nailed boards around the perimeter of the flat roof to catch rain. On the humid sunny days, he directed two fans toward the ceiling, and the trapped evaporating rooftop water gave the house a semblance of air conditioning. Jimmie and Carol shared one of the two bedrooms, snuggling into their respective bunk beds at night. After Carol died, they were allowed to rent a three-bedroom house. I suppose that was one way the government assuaged their guilt over my sister's death. The swing set was supposed to be staked into the ground and it wasn't.

As a production site for uranium 235, high security fences surrounded the entire city. Seven gates, complete with armed guards, allowed the population of seventy-five thousand to pass if they wanted to leave or enter the city. Everyone was required to wear an identity badge when they were outside their home. My eleven-year-old brother, Jimmie, proudly pinned his badge on his T-shirt and went outside to play one day. That was the day he found a hole under the security fence. He scampered home, grabbed his .22 rifle, returned to the hole, and wriggled under it. Then he camouflaged the hole with leaves and went squirrel hunting. So much for tight security.

Another day, my brother skipped down the boardwalk to the dump. There he found huge tomatoes growing, the seeds of which had apparently escaped the normal dump burning . . . and had possibly been irradiated. Being entrepreneurial, he harvested them and sold them to our neighbors, until they found out where the tomatoes had come from. Needless to say, his business venture was short-lived.

When my dad found work in Oak Ridge as an instrument maintenance man, he'd moved his family from Detroit. His work ended, however, in March 1947, after the nuclear bomb was dropped on Hiroshima. The workers at the secret city had completed their jobs without ever knowing what they were working on. Without the help of the Internet, Dad somehow found a job with the Diamond Alkali Company, and we moved to Perry, Ohio, thirty-five miles east of Cleveland, to an old farmhouse on five acres of lakefront property. I was nine months old.

I loved growing up in the country. Though I had a few dolls, I rarely played with them. Climbing to the top of a tree to survey the neighboring peach orchard was much more fun—and dangerous. I was Sheena, Queen of the Jungle, or more importantly, Wonder Woman, my main role model, striving for truth, justice, peace, and equality for women. She was confident, intelligent, and powerful, and a definite precursor to today's alpha female. I wanted to be just like her—fighting evil with her golden lasso of truth and bracelets that could stop bullets.

My father's parents were schoolteachers who had the summers off. They made good use of their time by vacationing all over the place, from Canada to Florida and from Michigan to California. There were no interstates in the twenties and thirties. I can only imagine the adventure they set out on every summer, their car loaded with several spare tires and camping equipment. They even camped their way to Yellowstone one summer and enjoyed the bears. When I was a kid, my parents carried on the tradition by always going somewhere on their vacations. We traveled the US, and I caught the travel bug—one for which there is no cure.

My mother was a stay-at-home mom until I started school. Then she found a job as a telephone operator for Ohio Bell Telephone Company, and later became a supervisor, getting home at five thirty. Dad got home at four thirty. The country school bus dropped me off by four, so by the time I was nine, I'd become a latchkey kid. Left to myself for a half hour, I'd climb to the top of my favorite tree. From that vantage point, I'd watch my father pull into our dirt driveway. I'd quickly climb down the tree and run to him. Rings of sweat always circled the armpits of his green work shirt, and the afternoon sun glistened on his balding head. He always reminded me of President Eisenhower.

"Daddy, Daddy, can we go swimming now? Huh?"

"Okay." He laughed. "Let me get changed into my swimming trunks. Go find our book and bring it with you. I'll be ready in a minute."

We sat on a huge log swept onto shore by a brutal winter storm that had blown in from Canada. The lure of the cool lake waters would have to wait, however, because recitation came first. I pulled *A Hundred and One Poems* from my bag.

"By the shores of Lake Erie, by the shining big sea water, stood the wigwam of Sue Ann, daughter of the moon, Nokomis." I proudly performed a customized version of Longfellow's "Hiawatha's Childhood."

Ever patient, and clearly amused, my father smiled slightly and said, "Recite it correctly, Sue Ann, otherwise you won't get your fifty cents. Start again." I laughed and did as he asked.

My father and I spent a lot of time on that log. He told me that when I grew up I could be anything I wanted to be. My proposed occupations, however, were gently shot down one after the other: boxer, fireman, doctor, minister, police officer, football player.

"Women don't box, Sue Ann. For one thing, little girls are built differently than little boys. They would get hurt if they boxed," he explained.

Rebuffed but hardly discouraged, I developed a simple solution to the problem my father posed: I would discover the secret strength of ants. I'd spent hours watching shiny black ants crawl in and out of their mound, carrying grains of dirt and leaves much larger than themselves. If I could discover their secret, I could bottle it and sell it. Maybe, with their strength, I'd be strong enough to box.

Me bathing in kitchen sink at age 5. Perry, Ohio.

After a particularly brutal winter, my family moved nine miles farther west to Painesville, where my mother worked, just before I started sixth grade. It was also a closer commute for my father to get to work at the stinky Diamond Alkali factory, which made chemicals. The stench spewing from the smokestacks made anyone who came within two miles of it wrinkle up their nose. My neighborhood girlfriends and I would take long bike rides, ending at a thick white soupy pond, surrounded by barren trees. I mean barren as in no leaves, no bark, no life. We poked the white mystical soup with sticks, but made sure we never got close enough to fall in. No huge tomatoes grew around that chemical dump.

To further amuse ourselves, we started a club—the SSS Club, or Silent Secret Service. How fortuitous, or was it? We pretended to be spies and hid in the basement root cellar gazing out a little window into the backyard watching for bad guys. The Wonder Woman inside of me was again fighting evil. A half century later, I think about the TV programs that held my interest at the time: *Sea Hunt*, a scuba-diving adventure; *77 Sunset Strip*, about two private detectives; *Adventures of Superman*, who fought for truth, justice, and the American way; and my favorite, *Maverick*, who, with his brother, played poker in the Wild West, but was extremely ethical and always chose doing the right thing over financial gain. I wonder which came first. Did I like those programs because I was already predisposed to justice, duty, courage, honesty, and loyalty, or did those TV shows influence my future endeavors?

Summers flew by as my friends and I created ways to entertain ourselves. These were the days of no cell phones, video games, or computers. With a spark of creativity, we wrote, directed, designed the set and costumes, and acted in a play, *Johnny Appleseed*, about an American folk hero who planted orchards of apple trees across Ohio and the Midwest. We charged twenty-five cents admission, and shared our $4.50 take from two performances.

My years at Harvey High School in Painesville were packed with every activity I could fit into my schedule, from French Club to Girls' Athletic Association. It was my way of keeping busy and not being bored. Under my father's patient teaching, I became a ham radio operator at thirteen, tapping out Morse code at five words a minute. By fourteen, I had my own laboratory set up in the basement, where I carefully sliced frozen chicken livers and stained them with gentian violet to observe their cellular structure under a microscope. Science fascinated me, but my high school advisor discouraged me pursuing a career as a medical technologist.

"Sue Ann, you're too much of a people person to be working in a lab alone." She was correct, though I didn't understand it at the time. I only had four really close friends: Beth Philipbar, Carol Thompson, Peggy Dieckow, and Linda Sarna. Beth was in the popular clique, but the rest of us resigned ourselves to the second most popular clique. We were the ones who didn't get asked to parties or to dance at the Saturday night YMCA Canteen. We'd impatiently wait for *ladies choice* to be announced and then try to summon enough courage to ask the popular boys to dance. I was just a flat-chested skinny ninth grader, still unsure of myself, and as boy crazy as any fifteen-year-old.

Every fall was kicked off with Harvey High School's annual magazine drive. It appealed to my competitive nature, and even in tenth grade, I quickly became one of the top sellers, winning prize after prize. It was so easy. Dad dropped me off at Lake Erie College for Women, and I went into the dorms and sold magazine subscriptions to wealthy, bored students. (In Painesville, we called it Lake College for Eerie Women.) None of the boys could have done it, and none of the other girls thought of it. Maybe I was a people person after all.

The summer between my senior year in high school and starting college at Ohio University, I worked as a telephone operator, sitting in a high swivel chair, deftly plugging and unplugging pairs of cords into rows of jacks. The switchboard looked like a plate of black spaghetti had been thrown against it. There was no automatic equipment capturing the calling or called number for billing purposes. As long-distance operators, we had to dial the numbers on a rotary dial, connect to the correct party, record the billing information on a stack of cardboard tickets, and disconnect the two correct pieces of spaghetti when a customer hung up. It was multi-tasking at its best. The tickets lay to the side of each operator's position. I would carefully mark the oval numbered boxes with my pencil to designate relevant information. As hard as I tried, though, I never completed a shift with perfectly marked tickets.

I was never perfect enough in my father's eyes, either. He would complement me on an achievement, but then his German heritage and strict teacher parents bubbled to the surface.

"Sue Ann, that's really good, but next time you could do it this way and make it better." In retrospect, I know he was a loving parent trying to teach me a better way, but what he created in me was the fear of failure—of never being quite good enough. His teaching was a double-edged sword. While it drove me to try harder to please him and do things perfectly, I gave up some dreams for fear I wouldn't accomplish them. I never did discover the strength of ants. Dreams are a terrible thing to lose.

I graduated from high school after my induction into the National Honor Society. I was smart and likable, but I still wanted to avoid any SAT college admission exams for fear of not passing them. I applied to and was accepted at Ohio University, which didn't require SATs. I was also following my high-school boyfriend, Chuck, who was attending OU and majoring in photography. It had been a rocky two-year relationship, but I was in love and determined to win him back. During high school, I'd been the head yearbook photographer, spending hundreds of hours in the darkroom developing black-and-white film and printing pictures. It was natural to choose photography as my major. There were only two problems: a photography major included a healthy dose of art classes, and I couldn't draw a stickman; and secondly, I realized I was not assertive enough to even direct my photo subjects. Changing majors, to interpersonal and organizational communications, I gravitated toward what I was good at with my gift of gab—speaking. I'd been the lead in the senior class play, *The Gazebo*, and I wasn't afraid of speaking to an audience. My assigned college faculty advisor, with a PhD after his name, taught several of my communication courses. We rarely saw eye to eye. Always practical, I questioned him one day about how the theory he was teaching was applicable to real life. He looked over his glasses, which were constantly sliding down his aquiline nose, and told me: "If you were a good student, Sue Ann, you would research it and figure it out." Perhaps I was an immature student. If I liked a professor or the subject, I worked hard and got As and Bs. If I didn't like the professor, I'd dig my heels in and not study. Of course, it was only me that I was hurting, but in my prideful stubbornness, I showed him.

I never won Chuck back. Instead I met Brad, a photojournalist, in my sophomore year and fell in love for a second time. Between our junior and senior year, we took advantage of a summer work program OU offered in Germany. My job was working with two- to five-year-old children at a state-run children's home. Totally submerged in the German language, I quickly crammed as much as I could into my head. The first whole sentence I learned to say was, "Wer hat in die Hosen gemacht?" or "Who made it in their pants?" This was my first taste of international travel and I was hooked. At the end of six work weeks, Brad and I bought a 1959 Opal and traveled through Germany, Switzerland, Austria, northern Italy, Monaco, France, and Belgium, all on fifteen dollars a day. In Ostend, he announced he was leaving me to go to England and look for relatives. There I was, stuck with a stick-shift car I didn't know how to drive and our camping equipment. *I can do this*, I thought, as the dang oil-guzzling car jerked down the road until I could get it into third gear. It was exciting to realize I could fend for myself in a foreign land and language. I spent seven days outside of Amsterdam in a campground with an eclectic mixture of young students from all over Europe and celebrated my twenty-first birthday.

The week before I graduated, I had my final consultation with my advisor, the good doctor, who glared at me and said, "Sue Ann, you are the worst student I've ever had. I doubt that you will ever amount to much." Anger filled my eyes with tears and I couldn't speak. I turned around and fled from his little cubicle, slamming the door behind me. My father's words came back to me: "You can do anything you want to do." I just needed to figure out what that was.

At the end of my senior year, with my C+ average and a winning smile, I attended a communications conference and was hired by University of Maryland as a part-time conference coordinator for their adult education division. My new boss not only offered me a job, but also found me an apartment and a woman to room with, who also worked at University of Maryland. My general four-year degree, along with a dime, could get me a cup of coffee. I was lucky to find a paying job and to have so much help making a transition into adult life. The only caveat was that I had to be in grad school, so I chose to start a master's program in public relations at American University. My parents helped me pack a small U-Haul trailer with all my worldly belongings and waved goodbye as I pulled out of the driveway and headed for Washington, DC. My only goal was to get on with my life and have an adventure, meet new people, and live in a different place. I was ready to tackle the world. One question still nagged at me, though. How was I going to make my life count?

Chapter 3:

December 1968: A Year Without the Right Job

During my tenure at University of Maryland, I coordinated a conference for Cleveland, Ohio, policemen who were having difficulty dealing with all the personnel and organizational changes going on in their department. I saw grown men break down and cry from the stress of the changes. It shocked me. I loved change and always embraced it. I couldn't believe anyone could get so upset, and vowed it would never happen to me. Many of the men encouraged me to think about becoming a policewoman. The seed was planted. All it needed was some water.

I dropped out of grad school because I didn't really

want to be there. That caused me to then quit my job at the university. I sought help from Frank and Faith Gallo, friends from my hometown in Ohio, who also lived in the DC area. They introduced me to Ray, who hired me as a headhunter. Ray taught me how to find engineers and system analysts who wanted to change jobs in the aerospace industry. I started to learn how to investigate and question people, and I was good at it. What I wasn't good at was accepting Ray's unethical business behavior of bedding corporate secretaries to get his hands on company phone directories. I never believed the end justifies the means. He gave me the directories, and I had to figure out how the departments were numerically coded, so we could call into the ones we wanted to raid. While I was paid well, paychecks were sporadic, and after a few months, it was time to move on. That's when I was exposed to the real world of job hunting and taking all those damned typing tests. In the late sixties and early seventies, when a woman went on a job interview, even with her four-year college degree in hand, she was first given a typing test. Men dictated and women took shorthand, or typed. It was never the other way around. Women had few career choices: teacher (not the professor), airline stewardess (not the pilot), nurse (not the doctor), Avon lady (not the CEO), secretary (not the COO), bookkeeper (not the accountant), maid (not the homeowner), or telephone operator (not senior management). Women were never paid the same as men even if they were doing the same job. Unbelievably, it's still the case today in many areas. The Women's Liberation movement was just beginning to raise awareness among women that they were being oppressed, and that they needed to band together in sisterhood. The 1968 Miss America pageant in Atlantic City set the stage for the first protest. Women's libbers made signs renouncing the beauty pageant contestants as nothing more than sheep being blindly led to the slaughterhouse to be butchered like meat. The media picked up on someone saying they were burning women's bras as a protest. While this never actually happened, it became a signature statement for the women's movement. What women really wanted to get rid of was the girdle. My mother wore one, and I remember watching her stuff her folds into it until they spilled over the top just beneath her bra. It was the first thing she took off when she came home after standing on her feet all day at the telephone office. The girdle's side zipper firmly left its imprint like train tracks in her soft skin. There is no question that it was a torture device, and guess what. It was invented around 1910 by a Frenchman named Paul Poiret. Need I say more? Although I'd never worn a girdle, with the advent of the women's movement, I shed my bra, too. Free at last. I never wore see-through blouses, but in cold weather my freedom was pretty apparent.

When I interviewed with the head of one labor union, a balding, pudgy middle-aged man, whose clothes were as wrinkled as a newborn baby's skin, it wasn't my college degree and previous jobs that impressed him, but my typing.

"Sue Ann, how would you like to work for me? You would get to travel and meet clients in different cities, go out to dinner with them—you know, *entertain* them."

I looked at him wide-eyed, shocked by what I'd just heard. "Is this an in-bed or an out-of-bed job?"

He smiled and said, "It's whatever you want to make it." So much for DC politics and labor union jobs. I was out the door and on to my next interview faster than you could say AFL-CIO.

Finally, a friend introduced me to Susan Moore Roberts, a Washington, DC, policewoman working on the sex squad at Metropolitan headquarters investigating rape cases. But that wasn't always her job. When she was first assigned to the squad, she was relegated to typing reports for several months until she pushed her supervisors to let her do actual investigative work. She was my inspiration. When Susan invited me to share a little farmhouse in Potomac, Maryland, with her and her three large Great Danes, I jumped at the chance to get out of my high-rise apartment and back into the country. Susan was known for her long silky brown hair that reached to her butt, and she relished being called the "sweetheart of the third floor" by her partner. She worked hard and made detective grade early in her career, much to the dismay of many men.

I was still job hunting when one day she said, "Sue Ann, you really should consider applying to the police department. They're hiring a lot of people right now, especially since so many Vietnam veterans are coming home."

The pay started at eight thousand dollars a year, and Susan said *maybe* she could get me on the sex squad.

Chapter 4:

September 1969: That's Officer Baker to You

The hot, sticky DC summer slowly morphed into a cold, snowy December winter as I morphed from a civilian into a newly graduated MPD officer. It didn't seem like it was difficult to get hired. I had my college degree, and that was the first requirement for a woman (not a man) to become a police officer. I suppose that was because they always assigned women to the youth division to deal with kids. I was hoping for something more challenging and juicy like the sex squad or homicide, but alas. The academy, in Anacostia, was housed in what had been intended as temporary Navy buildings during

WWII. It was still there in 1969. The dreary classrooms were filled with high-school student desks in which forty-five eager souls sat learning federal and District laws. There was minimal cooling in the summer and little heat in the winter. I accepted the offer from one of my fellow officers to wear his wool coat to keep warm. I learned later that the fact he was African American did not sit well with many of the southern whites in the class. I didn't care. I was not raised to be prejudiced and didn't perceive the kind gesture for more than what it was. Actually, it did my heart good to see one of the most racist white officers faint during a film on how to deliver a baby. There were two other macho cops who chose to leave the room. Good grief, it was only a film, and they weren't even the ones pushing that baby out.

I have vivid memories of my first day at the indoor range when it was explained to me how to hold the gun and line up the front sight in the middle of the back sight. "Now pull the hammer back and just slowly and steadily squeeze the trigger," the instructor said. "It should be a surprise when it goes off."

I concentrated hard, listening to the instructions. My left hand wrapped around my right as my fingers clenched the grip, my arms extended. I was raised shooting a .22 caliber rifle at empty cans bobbing in Lake Erie. How hard could this be? I squeezed the trigger slowly as the sights wove around the center of the target in a lazy horizontal figure eight.

BAM. It surprised me alright. Shocked and scared by the noise and the motion of the gun thrusting my hands upward with its recoil, tears welled up in my eyes. I was the only woman on the firing line. *Stop it. You can't cry now, Sue Ann. You're a cop. Cops don't cry.* The instructor behind me continued down the line of shooters. I don't think he saw how shaken I was. Composing myself, I pulled the hammer back and fired again, and again, and again. *I can do this.*

The day came when we were bused to a field where a large tent was set up. Dressed in our jeans and T-shirts, we stepped out of the bus and gathered around the sergeant.

"Listen up," he yelled in his baritone voice. The group immediately quieted down. He pointed to a pile of gas masks. "You will go over there and pick out a mask. This is how you put it on," he said demonstrating. "Make sure it fits tight around your face. You will then go in the tent, one after the other, and after thirty seconds, take off your mask. The tent is filled with C2 tear gas, and you will shout out your name and birthday. Do not close your eyes or the tear gas powder will get on your eyelids. Do not put the mask back on. You will exit the tent immediately. DO NOT wipe your eyes. Do you understand?" We all said, "Yes sir," and nervously picked out masks and lined up. I was tenth in line and watched in horror as guys came running out the other side of the tent coughing and choking. Trepidation washed over me, but I couldn't declare I wasn't going to do it. When my turn came, in I went. The inside of the tent was foggy white with tear gas. I stood there for a few breaths and realized that the mask was working. I was doing just fine until the sergeant motioned for me to take it off. I spit out my name and birthday as fast as I could. My eyeballs felt like an army of tiny needles was marching across them, and they immediately started watering. I stumbled out of the tent just like everyone else. It was the one time everyone cried.

Next, we all got to spend two days working with officers in different squads. I was assigned to the vice squad. It was an eye-opening experience. Two vice detectives decided to take me into a gay bar. I think they wanted to see my reaction, because they didn't tell me where we were going. We walked into the bar. It was dark, smoky, and people danced in the center of the room, while the jukebox played "Wedding Bell Blues" by the 5th Dimension. We made our way up to the bar and ordered soft drinks.

"Do you notice anything different in here, Sue Ann?" questioned the detective.

As my eyes adjusted to the dim light, I did indeed notice that men were slow dancing with men, and a woman at the end of the bar had her arm around another woman. They were also eyeing me with curiosity, or what I hoped was just curiosity. It was rare in those days that anyone came out of the closet, so my exposure to gay couples was nonexistent. "Yeah, is this a gay bar?"

Both detectives laughed at the expression of disbelief on my face. "Yes, it's one of the several in DC. We stop in here about once a week just to make our presence known. Come on, let's go. Next stop is a porn store."

While I was surprised by the gay bar, I was thoroughly embarrassed by what I saw for sale at the porn store. Case after glass case held handcuffs, whips, dildos of all shapes, colors, and sizes, vibrators, plus a few things I couldn't identify at all. I wanted to take my time and look, but I didn't want the detectives to see my curiosity. I did my best to look like I wasn't shocked, and casually walked around the store and then back to them as they were leaving. By the end of the night, I was pretty sure I didn't want to be on the vice squad.

I'd been given a good glimpse of what being a city cop was like, and I was eager to get started making a difference. Finally, on a sunny day in December, forty-five graduating cadets proudly posed for our class photo—twenty-five were black and twenty were white; only four of us were women.

Washington, DC Police Academy

Upon graduation, I received my assignment. You guessed it—Youth Division.

I basically grew up as an only child. My brother, Jim, was twelve years older than I and was out of the house by my seventh birthday. My closest playmate lived a half mile from me. Growing up in the country, on the shores of Lake Erie, I'd played mostly alone. I knew little about dealing with children, and nothing about dealing with teenagers or juvenile delinquents covered in heroin tracks. The cops on the beat would catch a kid committing a crime, like climbing through a second-story window to break into a house. It was amazing that the kid could come up with a somewhat reasonable explanation as to why he was on that roof. I couldn't have thought up the lies I heard if my life depended on it. The beat cops would leave the kid in my custody, often handcuffed to a chair while I took his statement. Then I, or another officer, would transport him to the detention center for holding until arraignment in juvenile court the next day. My lieutenant happened to be a tall, light-skinned African American woman. I'm sure she had worked very hard to rise to that position, and she was a perfectionist. Her background was as a teacher apparently, because she would grade me on my reports. They had to be typed perfectly on an original form, plus six copies, all at the same time. It was almost impossible to keep all the copies from moving around the typewriter roller while I painstakingly erased a mistake—seven times. Then I positioned carbon paper on top of all the pages so that when I hit the correct letter, it could be transferred to the copies. It was tedious work, and there I was typing after all.

My longest report concerned the arrest of four juvenile boys who had stolen a car and gone joyriding in a cemetery, crashing into headstones and knocking the heads off statues. They were ten and eleven and could barely see over the wheel of the car. They showed no remorse while admitting to their night of fun—only giggles and laughter. The damage was in the thousands of dollars, the paperwork horrendous, and they ultimately only got their hands slapped. I got compensatory overtime that I could use later when I wanted time off, and an A on my lengthy report.

My short tenure with the Metropolitan Police Department provided me with many new experiences: how to drive a squad car, how to talk on the police radio, how to step to the side of a door when knocking on it, how to present a court case, how to recognize heroin tracks, and how to write great just-the-facts-ma'am reports.

By the summer of 1970, however, I'd had enough of dealing with juveniles, or maybe I'd just had enough of being a city cop. It was also unclear how many years I would have to work in the youth division before I could get moved to another division. At that time, policewomen did not wear uniforms, nor did they work in the streets. The field was very limited, and Susan was the rare woman to escape the stationhouse and become a detective in the sex squad.

I also realized that I was becoming callous with my feelings, in an attempt to detach myself from the crime and child abuse I'd witnessed in the ghetto. It's a risk that comes with the job. It was easy to cross the bridge into Virginia to my white suburban high-rise apartment I'd moved to, overlooking the swimming pool. It wasn't easy to forget what I'd dealt with that day. A career fighting street crime isn't easy. One way or another, it takes a toll.

One payday, I decided I would treat myself to an actual restaurant lunch instead of my usual peanut butter cheese crackers and Coke out of the precinct vending machines. Sweat dribbled down my back, and little droplets emerged on my upper lip. I couldn't take being inside my precinct any longer that day. The smell of urine and sweat, and God knows what else, accumulated over almost a century of use, permeated the walls and assaulted my nose with unyielding pungency.

As I was crossing over K Street, I looked to my right and recognized John, an Executive Protective Service officer (EPS), strolling along beside me. I hadn't seen him since we were rookies together at the police academy. Now he worked at the White House.

"How's it going at the precinct, Sue Ann?"

I wrinkled up my nose and slightly shook my head. "How have you been doing?"

"Fine, just working shift work at the west gate. Why don't you come over to the White House and work with me?"

I resisted at first, saying, "You know there's no women officers at the White House."

He winked at me. "Times are changing, Sue Ann. With all the pressure to hire women these days, they're 'exploring possibilities.' If I were you, I'd go ahead and call the chief of police at the White House and tell him you're interested. When the positions are approved, you'll be top of the list."

I didn't grow up wanting to be an EPS Officer at the

White House. I had to admit, though, protecting the White House and embassies sounded much more glamorous than dealing with juvenile junkies and the District's criminal justice system. I reached out and took the scrap of paper with the name and phone number on it.

"OK, thanks. I'll call him." What did I have to lose?

Chapter 5:

December 1970: Welcome to the White House

I could hardly believe it when the captain's office called and scheduled an interview with me at the White House. I immediately called my parents to tell them the news. They were excited to think that their daughter could be working at the White House.

"What exactly would you be doing?" Mom asked.

"Well, I don't know for sure. I guess I'll be standing in the guard shacks around the White House like the men do. I'll let you know what they tell me."

"Do your best," my dad piped up. "We love you and are so proud of you." My heart smiled.

I remember it was a cool morning, in that short window of time between sunrise and the oppressive humidity and heat of a DC summer. I wore my white cotton suit with thin red and blue lines running through it that I'd sewn from a Simplicity pattern. I thought it was patriotic and would gain me some points. I swept my blond hair up in back, supporting a curly hairpiece. The traffic backed up as I neared downtown DC. Good thing I'd left plenty of time to get there and find a parking place three blocks from the White House. Here I was, a twenty-four-year-old woman from small-town Ohio, actually walking up to the East Portico of the White House. As I approached the guard shack, I tried to imagine myself standing there wearing a uniform with a gun at my side. I wondered if the uniform would be a skirt, or pants like the men.

I announced myself with all the calmness I could muster.

"My name is Sue Ann Baker and I'm here for an interview."

Checking the list on his clipboard in front of him, the guard said, "Yes, Miss Baker, you are expected. Follow the walkway to the first door. Officer Rodgers will be there to escort you to the interview room."

My nervousness rose as the officer led me down a plush red-carpeted arched hallway. White marble busts lined the hall. I swallowed hard and tried to breathe naturally. *You're not in Ohio anymore, Sue Ann.* We stopped at a heavy wooden door, and he knocked on it. A man in a suit opened it and welcomed me in, offering a seat at the head of the table. I sat down and clasped my hands on my lap under the table so no one would see them shaking. Two rather intimidating "suits" sat on either side of the table and stared at me. I remember one of them telling me that the interview was being tape-recorded, but I didn't see any tape recorder. It must have been in one of the walls, like in the Oval Office. They asked me questions about where I'd grown up, what college I had attended, how I came to be an MPD officer, and why was I applying for the position. They explained that the Executive Protective Service (EPS) was formerly called the White House Police, and was created in 1922. In 1930, it had been placed under the supervision of the Secret Service, and became the uniformed branch of the Secret Service. They gave me an official brief description of what the position required: "The EPS provides protection for the president and his family, the executive residence, grounds, and offices, and diplomatic missions in Washington, DC. An incumbent takes personal risk, is subject to irregular and extended hours of duty, and exposure to extremes of weather. He must become proficient in the use of firearms and must be able to perform a maximum efficiency at indoor standing posts, outdoor posts, walking patrol, and vehicular patrol."

They also explained that because of the Hatch Act of 1939, any political aspirations I might have, or activities with partisan political campaigns, were prohibited. This was true for other federal organizations such as the FBI, CIA, NSA, and many others. The act would be amended in 1993 to allow most federal employees to take part in partisan political campaigns or management. The list of do's and don'ts is still different for the Secret Service and other specific agencies. I told the suits that the restrictions would not be a problem for me. Although I was raised a Republican, I had little interest in politics.

The carrot at the end of the stick was the possibility of becoming a Secret Service agent in six months to a year. This was a pilot program designed to determine if women could function as agents, because we would be doing the same job as the male agents.

After the interview, they thanked me for coming and said they would be in touch in few days as they were interviewing other women. The wait was excruciating. The idea of actually changing jobs and working around the White House had been a dream. Now the possibility was real, and I wanted the opportunity badly. Finally, I received the happy phone call extending me the offer to formally apply to become an EPS officer. I filled out a lot of paperwork in which I listed references spread all over the country for my top-secret clearance, took an eye exam and a hearing test, and got a civil service physical exam. Among the functional and environmental requirements that were circled on the form for the physical exam were:

Ability for rapid mental and muscular coordination simultaneously

Ability to use and desirability of using firearms

Working around moving objects or vehicles

Working closely with others

Working alone

Protracted or irregular hours of work

I don't think I ever read the fine print on that form. I just turned in my papers and waited.

And waited. What was taking them so long, I wondered.

My swearing-in as an Executive Protective Service Officer, December 12, 1970

Finally, after six months, I was officially informed that I'd been hired as one of the first seven female Executive Protective Officers, along with Phyllis Shantz, Judy Michelsen, Holly Hufschmidt, Laurie Andersen, Kathryn Clark, and Denise Ferrenz. We were sworn in at different times and never did anything as a group. Phyllis, the first female ever to be sworn in as a federal law enforcement officer, says she doesn't remember any of the rest of us being around the White House.

We all were anxious to become US Secret Service Agents, but that would come in time. This was the first cautious step taken by a 105-year-old male bureaucracy facing the fact that times were changing.

Our first challenge was to gain the respect of the men and show them we could do a good job. However, considering that no one apparently ever thought to buy us uniforms, so we could do the same job as the men, it was almost impossible. They wouldn't let us stand post in the guard shacks around the White House, because, they said, no one would recognize the authority of someone in a dress. I remember being measured for a uniform, but time passed and I never got one. We worked for a year without ever having the right clothes.

I was assigned to do payroll and watch TV monitors and alarms systems in the Executive Office Building (EOB) next door to the White House.

Waiting for an alarm to go off was about as exciting as watching cold molasses drip off a spoon. In the basement of the EOB, I'd adjust my chair in front of the TV console to get comfortable and work on a huge needlepoint scene of a German town. It was my first needlepoint project. The other officers didn't seem to mind. They'd be busy talking about sports or doing the Sunday *New York Times* crossword puzzle.

It was boring, but it was a job, and my female colleagues and I were slowly becoming part of the boys' club—or so I thought.

Chapter 6:

March 1971: My First Big Gig—Protecting PM Lon Nol of Cambodia

"Congratulations, Sue Ann, you're going to Hawaii," exclaimed my sergeant. I looked at him in disbelief as he waved a paper in front of my face.

"What? Did I win a contest?"

"No, you're relieving Judy Michelsen, who has been there a little over a month protecting Sovanna Nol, wife of Cambodia's prime minister, Lon Nol. Lon Nol had a stroke, and the US government flew them to Hickam Air Force Base in Honolulu so he can get treatment. He's been a friend to the US and has allowed our planes to land in Cambodia during the war in Vietnam. It's in our interest to keep him alive and in power."

"How long will I be there?"

"I don't know. Guess you'll be there until he's well enough to go back to Cambodia. You'll need to see Bill Paine, Special Agent in Charge of the detail, for more information. He's flying over to relieve Doug Duncan."

I took the paper from his hand and scanned it briefly. My eyes landed on the departure date—the next day. I was so excited; my mouth must have looked like it had a coat hanger in it. I couldn't stop smiling. I'd never been to Hawaii, or even to the West Coast.

I met Bill Paine at Secret Service Headquarters. He was tall, distinguished looking, silver haired, and had a deep announcer-type voice. He also smoked like a fiend. Being around him certainly didn't help me kick my habit.

"Pack summer clothes, Sue Ann. I don't know how long we'll be there, but it's in the eighties. Take a bathing suit, too, cause Doug told me that Lon Nol's cottage is right across from a swimming pool. Our flight leaves out of National Airport at 1300 hours. Do you have your GTR?"

"Uh, I don't know. What's a GTR?" I asked.

"It's a government travel request that you can fill out and use to get your airline ticket, but maybe no one gave you a set of them because you're not an agent. I can use one of mine to pay for your ticket. And by the way, we'll be flying first-class since it's a nonstop eleven-hour flight to Honolulu, and you'll have to get to work when we land. Meet me at noon by the United ticket desk."

"Yes, sir. I'll see you then."

I jumped in my car and fought traffic all the way home to Virginia. My feet flew two steps at a time up to my second-floor apartment. Unlocking the door, I threw my purse and keys on the kitchen counter, looked around, and started giggling. The joy of travel coursed through me. I pulled my suitcase out of my closet and laid it on the bed, trying to figure out what to take. I threw in one paisley polyester pantsuit I hadn't seen for months. Rummaging around in the back of my closet, I found some more summer clothes and my bathing suit. Then I called my parents.

"Hi, Mom. Is Dad there?"

"Hi, honey. No, he's at chess club tonight. What's up?"

"Oh, well, guess where I'm flying to tomorrow."

"I have no idea. Where?"

"I going to Hawaii with the Secret Service to protect the prime minister of Cambodia and his wife. He's the guy who started the coup and overthrew Prince Siha-nouk about a year ago. He's had a stroke, and since he's a friend to the US, we've flown him to Honolulu for med-ical treatment. I don't know how long I'll be gone."

"Oh, Sue Ann, that's great news. Please write us and let us know what you're doing and when you'll be home. Will you be alone with them or will there be oth-er agents?"

"There's a whole detail assigned to protect Lon Nol, but I don't know how many guys, maybe eight or ten. I hope someone tells me what I'm supposed to do. May-be they'll just have me stand post behind a house. Who knows? I'll write, I promise. Gotta go finish packing. Love you."

"We love you, too. Be careful," my mom said with a catch in her voice.

I hung up the phone and took a deep breath. My excitement was too great to get caught up in her motherly concern. Turning on the stove burner, I poured myself a glass of Rhine wine and took a pan of Jiffy Pop popcorn from the cupboard. The aluminum foil slowly expanded as the corn popped. When it looked like a silver bald head from outer space, it was done. There was no time to cook a real meal. I had to eat, finish packing, and try to get a good night's sleep.

The next morning, parking at the airport, I lugged my heavy suitcase into the terminal. There was no such thing as a suitcase with wheels, no luggage inspection, no requirements to arrive two hours early, and no bags of peanuts and pretzel sticks substituting a real meal. Ah, those were the days. Many times, I arrived at my gate only ten minutes before they shut the door. That morning, I was right on time to meet Bill Paine as directed, and we picked up our tickets. Settling into our first-class seats, we were handed a mai tai and macadamia nuts. I was so impressed by the whole experience, I wrote my parents, *Dinner was fish amandine, steak, peas and mushrooms, potatoes, sweet dough bread, and a hot fudge sundae. Then came the movie Hell Boats, which was bad and I promptly fell asleep for one and a half hours.*

It was pouring when we finally landed and dashed for a taxi to drive us to Hickam Air Force base. I was shown to my VIP quarters—quarters that were usually reserved for generals. Maybe being the only woman on the detail had its advantages. My suite had two connecting rooms—a bedroom and a full living room complete with a wicker bar, coffee table, cane chairs, and a TV. Adjoining it was a fully equipped and stocked kitchen with a lei of flowers in the refrigerator. I took it out and laid it on the counter. Within minutes, the scent of plumerias wafted through the room as the flowers warmed. I kicked off my shoes, digging my toes into the plush gold shag carpeting. Even the bathroom was carpeted. *I could get used to this*, I thought. (Later I learned that four dollars of my fifteen-dollar per diem were deducted for the room. It was worth it.) I quickly changed my clothes, checked my gun, and headed out the door to pull my first shift.

I didn't have to stand post guarding a back door. Instead, another agent and I sat in the white limousine in front of Lon Nol's cottage and listened to the rain pelt the windshield. They were tucked in for the night and not expected to leave, but still, we were vigilant. The cottage inside an Air Force Base was secured whether or not they were in it, including during the night. I didn't know the guy I was working with, but we had two hours to get to know each other. It was always the same whether sitting on surveillance or on a protection detail. Conversations meandered through our professional or personal lives, our thoughts on current events, or dreams of the future. After we'd spent two hours trying not to doze off, two other agents arrived to relieve us and told me to get some sleep. No one had to tell me twice. With a five-hour time difference, my body thought it was three a.m.

It had been a very long day.

By the next morning, the rain had let up. I found the base mess hall and quickly ate my forty-five-cent breakfast of scrambled eggs, ham, hashbrowns, and a glass of milk. I didn't know what the day held for me, and I wasn't going to go hungry if I could help it. I returned to my quarters, nervously dressed, and almost sprinted past the landmark seventeen-story water tower, down the wide palm tree-lined streets to the cottage. I'd been told little about the Nol's background. I knew they were Buddhists, but I didn't know anything about that religion. Lon Nol, I was told, was a very humble man who loved to sit and look at trees and flowers. Madame Nol, twenty-seven, had been his concubine for years and clearly doted on him. He was thirty years her senior. They'd married only the year before but already had four children together.

Just as I reached the cottage, I looked down and realized that the hem was falling out of my dress. I was mortified, but there was no time to fix it. I stepped into the cottage, smiling as the prime minister and his wife slowly crossed the room toward me. Maybe if I could hold their gaze, they wouldn't see my ruined hem. Madame Nol was attractive and shy. I knew she didn't speak English, so I greeted her with "Good morning" in my best hastily learned Cambodian: "Arun sous-dey."

She seemed happily surprised and smiled gently. Prime Minister Nol complimented me, through an interpreter, on my pronunciation. I was glad we were off to a good start. I had been told that Madame Nol was not supposed to talk to anyone except her husband, unless it was in an official capacity, because of her position. However, over the next few days, she warmed up to me and tried to communicate in French, but her French was as bad as mine. We laughed a lot and held hands while we walked, as is the custom in her country. Though of course I obliged, my hands itched to be loose and ready. What if I had to get to my gun? It was all the way at the bottom of my purse. I wrote my parents, *I'm learning several words in Cambodian which the Madam delights in. The Prime Minister's doctor, who speaks the best English, gave me a Cambodian name meaning "pretty girl." They all get a big kick out of it now when I respond to being called that.*

Lon Nol, Sovanna Nol, and me in Hawaii.

Every morning, I'd ride in the follow-up car as the short motorcade made its way to the hospital where Lon Nol was receiving physical therapy. His left arm and wrist hung limp and he wore a leg brace, but he could walk short distances. Once the physical therapy was finished, we'd drive him back to his cottage for a rest and I'd have a couple of hours of free time. Along with a few of the other agents, I'd swing by the base pool to get some sun and cool off before meeting the prime minister and his wife for their afternoon ride around Oahu.

I was lucky to work the day shift and have my evenings free. One night, a tall blond-haired Texas agent, complete with drawl, invited me to have dinner with him at the Monkey Bar in Pearl City. The bar had been there since 1939 and had survived the attack on Pearl Harbor. I didn't know what to expect other than a tropical bar and was shocked to see little monkeys scrambling from tree branch to tree branch behind a glass partition. We sat at the bar and had a drink and a wonton appetizer while we watched the monkeys. Their antics were hysterical. After dinner, we walked upstairs to the rooftop and saw row upon row of bonsai trees. I had never seen any before and was amazed at their age and size. Some were fifty to one hundred years old, yet only eighteen inches tall.

The air was getting chilly, so we hailed a cab and called it a night. It was fun getting off the base and having dinner with Mr. Texan. We said goodnight when the taxi dropped me off in front of my quarters. No kiss goodnight, no drama, just mutual respect. It wasn't always that way.

One weekend, Lon and Sovanna Nol took a three-hour ride through the pineapple fields to the other end of the island. I stared out the window at the lush greenery and gorgeous water, a far cry from the midsummer sights and smells of the DC precinct. I felt like I'd hit the jackpot. I was actually getting paid to be in Hawaii. While I was certainly aware of my duty, it seemed like a vacation. I was seeing and learning new things just like on those two-week summer vacations I'd taken with my parents. We'd only visited the eastern part of the US and Canada. Now I was in paradise, and also ready to take a bullet for a couple I did not even know. Paradise and bullets didn't go together in my mind. However, it was a potential reality that I could not let myself forget. It was the duty I'd signed up for, and hopefully, I'd have the courage to follow through if the time came. On one level, the young human mind has a wonderful way of adopting an it-won't-happen-to-me attitude. At twenty-four, mine was in full gear.

As the motorcade pulled into a lookout at the beach, Lon Nol got out and slowly made his way toward the water. It was obvious he was tired. He'd looked at the beach for only a few minutes when our radio cackled and Bill Paine announced that Lon Nol wanted to go back to his cottage. I'm sure Lon Nol thought that paradise and rehab didn't go together, either.

Lon Nol, Sovanna Nol, and me in Hawaii. Unknown agent to the left.

Shortly before they were scheduled to return to Cambodia, he decided he wanted to fly in a helicopter. It was important to him to be able to get into and out of a helicopter, as he would be expected to do when he returned to his home country. He wanted to appear strong and in charge.

Ducking low under the whirling blades the day of the helicopter ride, I climbed into the military helicopter and sat behind Sovanna Nol. It was loud! I could hardly contain my excitement as the craft rose from the ground. I thought, *How lucky can a girl be?* We circled Diamond Head, a 760-foot crater and state monument, a few minutes east of Waikiki. No one talked during the flight as the noise from the chopper blades was deafening, even through our ear protection. We looked out the tiny windows and embraced the beauty of the sparkling

Hawaiian waters. Touching back down, Lon Nol carefully climbed out of the copter with a big grin on his face.
He'd done it. He was almost ready to go home and lead
his country.

Lon Nol getting in a helicopter.

The last thing he needed before he went home was
the stamp of approval from his American doctors. Several examined him one last time, including a doctor
flown in from Walter Reed Hospital in DC. Nol had come
as far as he could with his physical therapy in the two
months he'd been in Hawaii. None of his doctors wanted to take the risk of a carotid artery operation to clean
out the calcium deposits in his neck. It was a new proce-
dure, and there was always the possibility that he could
have another stroke. With nothing left to do, the doctors gave him their stamp of approval; he was free to go
home. The night before he left, a few agents and I were
invited to a farewell dinner at the House of Hong on Ka-
lakaua Street in Waikiki, hosted by Lon Nol's doctor and

one of his generals. I had never seen so much food that I couldn't identify, nor sat at a round table, the center of which was a large lazy Susan. The general kept slowly turning it while we all served ourselves. As a picky eater, my plate was certainly not full, but I managed to get through the meal and kept smiling. When dinner was finished, someone took a photo of the general, the general's *companion*, and me along with three Cambodians standing behind us.

Lon Nol's general in the middle, me on the right, others unknown.

As I prepared to leave my assignment, Lon Nol asked to see me. He thanked me for helping his wife and extended an invitation to visit them someday in Phnom Penh. He said he would provide a cottage for me to live in, servants, and an interpreter. Unfortunately, I never got the chance to take him up on his offer. The Khmer

Rouge, followers of the Communist Party in Cambodia, took over the country in 1975. Lon Nol and his wife climbed into his helicopter and fled the country, first to Hawaii and then to California, where they remained in exile until his death in 1985. In four years, the Khmer Rouge tortured and murdered an estimated two to three million Cambodian people.

In 2014, I sent for my Secret Service personnel file and for the first time saw this commendation, which had never been given to me.

July 16, 1974

Dear Mr. Rowley [Director of the Secret Service],

The performance of the members of the Secret Service assigned to duty in connection with the hospitalization and recuperation of Prime Minister Lon Nol of Cambodia was so superior as to merit special recognition . . . Agents Sue Baker and Judy Michelsen were also most thorough in their ministrations. Their thoughtfulness and consideration in the protection of Madame Lon Nol emphasized their flawless performance of duty.

—Admiral John S. McCain Jr., US Navy and Commander in Chief, Pacific Command (CINPAC)

Admiral McCain was commander of all the US forces in Vietnam from 1968–1972, and his personal relationship with Lon Nol most likely prompted the letter and his appreciation.

I had survived my first protective assignment. I don't know how someone decided I was ready. Perhaps Judy and I were simply being tested, since the risk of an assassination was low on the Air Force base, plus we were never alone with our protectee, Madam Nol. We definitely got a good dose of on-the-job training. The other agents I worked with teased me sometimes, but it was good-natured, not malicious. I was a novelty in their eyes, and I knew it. I did not want to screw up for myself or as a reflection on the other six women trainees. While we rarely saw each other, we were all absolutely unified in the desire to succeed. As for me, I couldn't wait to be sent on another protective assignment. Who knew where it would be the next time?

Chapter 7:

September 1971: Bright Lights, Big City, Birthing Tips

I'd just finished another boring eight-hour shift at the Executive Officer Building and was headed home, weaving my way through the busy streets of Washington, DC, in my little yellow 1969 Volkswagen. As I unlocked the door to my Arlington, Virginia, apartment, I heard the phone ringing. Throwing my gun-laden purse on the couch, I reached for it and answered, hoping it was a guy I had met at a Georgetown bar the night before.

"Hello, Sue Ann. This is Jerry Parr, Assistant Special Agent in Charge of the Foreign Dignitary Protective Division. I heard you did a good job with Lon Nol in Hawaii."

"Thank you, sir."

"We've got a protective detail headed for New York City tomorrow. We just learned last night that the Malaysian Prime Minister, Tun Abdul Razak, is bringing his wife, Rahah Noah. They're from Kuala Lumpur. Pack your bags. There's a flight out at six thirty you can catch to New York. Take a cab from the airport to the Waldorf Astoria. Report to Sam Spade, detail leader. You'll find him in room 1902 in the Tower. Any questions?"

"Do you know how long I'll be there?"

"They're planning on staying seven days, but you never know when plans can change. Anything else?"

"No, sir. Thank you."

Hanging up, I cracked my atlas and found Malaysia south of Vietnam, bordering Thailand. Kuala Lumpur was the most populous city in the country. I realized that meeting the Prime Minister and his wife might be another exotic adventure. I didn't even know what language they spoke. The world was a much larger place then than it is now.

On September 22, 1971, I arrived at LaGuardia Airport in Queens and took a cab to the Waldorf in Midtown Manhattan. It was (and still is) billed as one of the grandest hotels in the world. Opened in 1931, it was the tallest and largest hotel in the world, quickly becoming *the* place to stay. Marilyn Monroe used to live there in 1955 in a suite that cost a thousand dollars a week. In 1971, Ella Fitzgerald, the Queen of Jazz, sang at the Waldorf's Starlight Roof. Known for its art deco style, no two rooms were alike. Needless to say, I was a long ways from Ohio. The little 1100-square-foot cement block house I'd grown up in had none of the Waldorf's grandeur—no marble, elegant flowers, or statues. There must have been other agents as intimidated and awestruck by the opulence they saw, but no one discussed it. As I continued through my career, grand hotels became second nature to me. Like they say, though, you never forget your first one. I made my way through the lobby and up the tower elevator to find the command post. This is a room usually next door to the protectee's suite where agents can rest between posts. It acts as a radio center for communications, monitoring emergencies and keeping the agents in contact with one another.

When I stepped into a smoke-filled room full of male agents and communications men, all talking and laughter stopped. The men looked at me curiously. It is likely some of them had not met a female EPS Officer before. We'd been sworn in less than a year before.

I held out a hand to the detail leader. He tentatively shook it. "Hi, I'm Sue Ann Baker. I was told to report here."

"We've been expecting you. I'm Sam, the detail leader. You'll be with the prime minister's wife from the time she exits the suite until she returns, or until she joins her husband for the evening."

I nodded, feeling the other agents' eyes roving over my purse, my shoes, and my dress.

"At that time, the prime minister's detail will take over the responsibility of protecting her." He turned to an agent wearing a charcoal-gray suit. "This is Dan. You'll be working with him. It's just the two of you with Mrs. Razak. Her first stop today will be the Kennedy Child Study Center on Sixty-Seventh Street. At one, she'll go to lunch somewhere, but I don't know where. I think she wants to go shopping after that. Have you checked into your room?"

"Yes, sir, I have."

"Good. When she comes out of her suite, I'll introduce you to her and her staff. An embassy limo and follow-up car will drive all of you to the Kennedy Child Study Center. Any questions?"

"Will she be with her husband at all today?" I asked.

"No, he has an appointment with photographers at ten thirty and then lunch with David Rockefeller, a meeting at the United Nations, and a stag dinner tonight with the foreign minister of Thailand at the St. Regis. I don't know what she is doing for dinner. You'll have to play it by ear."

My head was swimming with details. There was so much to keep track of, and in a city as big and busy as New York.

"You have your radio, so keep in touch. Check in when you arrive and depart from a location. Oh, and Sue Ann, stay close to her."

I was beginning to feel overwhelmed by the task assigned to me, even though I knew there would be a New York field office agent with me. By now, the men in the room had started talking to each other again. A couple of them even came over to introduce themselves. I was never completely sure what was really behind those smiles, so I just smiled back and tried to act professional.

At ten thirty sharp, Mrs. Razak came out of her suite and Sam introduced her. She smiled and extended her hand. I shook it and couldn't help noticing the two-carat diamond on her index finger. Her grip was strong for such a small woman. She wore a long silk dress, with her medium-length dark hair pulled back from her cherubic round face. She was one beautiful, classy lady.

After touring the Kennedy Child Study Center, we ate lunch at a tiny Japanese restaurant. Then she requested to go to Bergdorf Goodman on Fifth Avenue. As our two-car motorcade pulled up to the front door, I hurried out of the follow-up car and waited. Agent Dan opened the door for Mrs. Razak and two other ladies. As we walked into the store, I was overwhelmed by opulence. This was a thousand steps above Sears Roebuck. Wide carpeted aisles and minimal displays gave it a classy look. The mannequins were draped in filmy, bejeweled cocktail dresses, held champagne glasses, and lounged on antique couches. Stuffed peacocks sat between them. One of the women seemed to know exactly where she was going, and we headed straight for evening bags. As I recall, Mrs. Razak bought at least four of them, priced around four hundred dollars each. That's $2345 apiece in 2014 dollars. I marveled how anyone could spend that kind of money on one purse. Besides, I could never fit my gun in the evening bags like she was buying. As we maneuvered through the store looking at different things, I'd never felt more like a small-town girl. This was a whole new world to me and a far cry from the time I'd spent arresting teenage heroin addicts in DC.

Next stop was Bloomingdale's, where she continued

to shop until four thirty. When we arrived back at the Waldorf, I had two hours off until we left for the Palace Theater, where the musical *Applause* starring Anne Baxter was on. Mrs. Razak requested that I sit with her in the sixth row. Being in a dark theater made me more than a little vigilant. Dim lights and big crowds made potential threats less visible. I was on high alert for the whole show.

After the play, we headed to a Chinese restaurant. The women again asked me to sit with them while the male agent took a seat at a table nearby. While they chatted, I kept my eyes on our surroundings, seeking out anyone who looked out of place—someone nervous, under- or overdressed, with their hands in their pockets, a loner, someone who kept staring in our direction. My attention was diverted, however, when one of the women wanted to explain to me how new mothers in Malaysia had their stomachs bound tightly for a month or two after giving birth. Various herbs and oils were placed against their skin, and then a cloth would be wound tightly around their stomachs to make fat and stretch marks disappear. I thanked them for the information and promised to remember it if I ever decided to have children (which I didn't). We arrived back at the hotel at eleven thirty. As I left Mrs. Razak at her suite door, I breathed a sigh of relief. The day had ended without incident. I promptly returned to my room and fell into bed, exhausted after a sixteen-hour shift.

I had been excited to see NYC, but after a week, I was ready to get back DC and see the rolling hills of Virginia. The aggressive, macho manner of the New York agents and city cops made me feel like a fish out of water, and I decided right then, I never wanted to live there. There was no way of knowing then that I would soon spend a long, hot summer in Brooklyn.

Chapter 8:

October 1971: For the Love of Tito

Six months later, in October, Yugoslavian president Josip Broz (nicknamed Tito) and his wife, Jovanka Broz, flew into DC for a state visit with President Nixon. Tito had welcomed Nixon's visit to Yugoslavia the previous year—the first visit ever made by an American president. Nixon was returning the hospitality, continuing to build relations with Tito as a conduit to Egypt and the Middle East.

A communist dictator, Tito held six republics together for thirty-five years: Slovenia, Croatia, Bosnia-Herzegovina, Serbia, Montenegro, and Macedonia. He sought relations with the west while denouncing Stalin in

Russia, but always maintained a non-aligned status, preserving diplomatic neutrality between the two superpowers. When Tito died in 1980, presidents, prime ministers, kings, and dictators attended his funeral as Yugoslavians wept for the man they viewed as father of their county. Eleven years later, as nationalism arose, wars started among the Muslims, Croats, and Serbs who used to live next to each other in relative peace under Tito.

In 1971, Phyllis Shantz and I were charged with protecting Tito's wife. Every head of state has their friends and enemies. While many people in the US loved him, we had to keep in mind that friendly crowds could be as dangerous as angry ones. I didn't know anything about Yugoslavian politics, but I figured it would behoove me to at least know where in the world Yugoslavia was— back to the atlas. Agents are apprised of pertinent intelligence information on visiting diplomats, particularly if there are security concerns, but there was no special training on world geography or world politics. It seemed reasonable to know *something* about the person I was protecting.

It was a beautiful autumn day when President Nixon greeted Tito on the red-carpeted south lawn of the White House for Tito's first official state visit. Both presidents reviewed the military troops standing at attention. At the end of the ceremony, Nixon threw his arm around him and shouted, "Zivela Yugoslavia!" (Long live Yugoslavia!). In response, Tito turned to him and said, "Viva America." Both men were creating a legacy as international politicians.

Mrs. Broz, Tito Broz, President Nixon, and Pat Nixon at the White House.

Mrs. Broz, a rather large woman, was perfectly coiffed and dressed, but she still looked like the spitting image of my childhood vision of a Communist woman. All she needed was a peasant dress and a babushka tied around her head. That was the image I saw in the old news reels of Eastern Europe aired on TV in the fifties. As we traveled with them in the next few days, Phyllis and I both remember how gracious she and Tito were to everyone, including the Secret Service agents.

On October 30th, we flew from DC to Houston so Tito could visit NASA's Manned Spacecraft Center (now the Johnson Space Center). I rode in the Eastern Airlines plane with the press and the Yugoslavian security. A rather short young security agent tried to speak to me with the few words he knew in German, then French, and then English, accentuating with gestures. For a few moments, I couldn't understand what he was trying to tell me, but when he pursed his lips as if to kiss me, it became clear.

I laughed. "No, but thank you," I said, first in German then in French. It wasn't the first time I had ever been hit on by someone speaking a foreign language, and it wouldn't be my last. Guess you can't blame a guy for trying.

When we landed in Houston, it was apparent that the advance agent had done his job. He'd flown to Houston several days ahead of Tito's visit to arrange security with the local Secret Service office and local and state police. Barricades were raised; schedules were coordinated; locations were assessed; routes were driven to the nearest hospital; communications and a command post were set up at the Houston Oaks Hotel; background checks were run on hotel staff; Tito's hotel suite was swept for bombs and listening devices; lapel pins were issued in different colors depending on the person's position—the list was almost endless. The only thing he'd forgotten to do was turn down the heat. Even in October, Houston was stifling as we exited the airplane.

The advance agent had arranged for a black Cadillac limousine to carry Tito and his wife to the hotel. It was waiting at Ellington Air Force Base when we landed, followed by an array of cars for the motorcade. Large numbers of Houston police and sheriff's deputies had been enlisted to shore up security. The highways had been totally cleared of traffic. After getting settled at the Houston Oaks, we left for a tour of the Manned Spacecraft Center.

When we arrived, we were greeted by Robert Gilruth, the director of the Center, and astronaut Thomas Stafford. I stood at the back of a small group of people crowded into Mission Control while Tito was shown an Apollo spacesuit. He seemed impressed by it and, through interpreters, asked many questions. He even joked that he would like to try it on sometime, but that going to space wasn't for him.

The next day, Tito and his party flew to Palm Springs. There were hundreds of friendly people waiting to greet him at the airport. An enormous crowd pressed forward to shake his hand. You would have thought he was a Kennedy. Phyllis grabbed the wrists of agents on either side of her to form a human chain blocking the crowd. One of the male agents ridiculed her, questioning why she was in the inner defense line when she wasn't strong enough. Phyllis gritted her teeth and held tight. The barrier worked. I stayed close to Mrs. Broz as we made our way to the waiting limousine.

The Brozes spent the night at the secluded estate of Leonard Firestone, son of Henry Firestone, the tire magnate. A seven-thousand-square-foot villa built in 1950 was the perfect rest stop for them. The fact that it was secluded made it easier to secure by setting up perimeter posts around the complex. When they were safely tucked in for the night, I had a few hours free to explore Palm Springs. I wrote a postcard to my parents: *Palm Springs is fantastic, so much nicer than LA. Everything is expensive though. Getting my hair done now. Couldn't stand it. We're flying an Eastern chartered plane with the press and Yugoslavian security. Leaves before their plane so we just stay ahead of him. Am tired. Wish I could stay here a week.* No such luck. We were off to LA the next morning.

Tito's trip ended there. A luncheon was held by the World Affairs Council at the Century Plaza Hotel. Two thousand people heard his only major speech during his weeklong visit, in which he urged the US to embrace the United Nations as the best way to promote peace and to help those countries that are in "a sea of poverty and want." Later that evening, he and Mrs. Broz attended a reception hosted by Mayor Sam Yorty and the Association of Motion Picture and Television Producers. The next day, they boarded a plane for Canada and another adventure came to a close.

I was fortunate to have Phyllis on the detail. We usually worked different shifts, which gave both of us a little time off. When we had a chance to exchange notes, we concurred that our whirlwind trip across the United States had given us more protective experience, and practice handling large crowds—larger than I'd experienced.

"I wonder if they'll ever make us agents and give us the training other agents have. It's tough to have any credibility when we're not really agents," Phyllis complained.

"Yeah, you got that right," I nodded in agreement.

Part II:

Special Agents

Chapter 9:

December 15, 1971: The Titanic is Not Sinking

By the following December, all seven of us had rotated through various temporary assignments protecting female foreign dignitaries. Yet, we'd still had no formal Secret Service training, beyond learning how to use a firearm. We wondered just how long we would have to prove ourselves before the Secret Service would fully accept us as agents. Executive Protective Service officers especially were jealous because we got to travel and dress more casually, while they stood guard in their crisp, starched uniforms around the White House. After almost a year, there was talk of mutiny among us. I don't know if any of us would have quit at that point, but we were not happy. I wanted to get back on the street and do investigative work. We wanted to be fully trained Secret Service agents as we'd been promised.

Bureaucratic wheels turned slowly, but finally it was our day. I had never been given a written performance review, and I have no idea how the final decision was made, but in retrospect, I think agents Charlie Gittens, Jerry Parr, and Clint Hill had a lot to do with it. The Department of Treasury sent out a press release and short biographies on each of us: Laurie Andersen, 24; Phyllis Shantz, 25; Holly Hufschmidt, 28; Kathryn Clark, 24; and Sue Ann Baker, 25. We were all single and had all been DC Metropolitan police officers, with the exception of Kathy Clark, who had worked for a congressman.

By that time, Judy Michelsen was married and pregnant, and was not offered an agent position. Officer Denise Ferrenz had not served as an EPS officer for a full year. She came aboard within a few months as the sixth female agent.

On December 15, 1971, we broke through the 106-year-old glass ceiling of what had been a tight-knit male fraternity as "we girls" filed into room 4121 in the Main Treasury Building to take our place in history.

Special Agent Ken Thompson proclaimed, "This is a day that will go down in infamy—like the sinking of the Titanic, the San Francisco earthquake, or the bombing of Pearl Harbor." Dozens of cameras flashed and the male reporters chuckled as we stood there, feeling self-conscious and wondering whether or not to laugh. With our backs to the news cameras, to hide our identities, we raised our right hands and were administered the oath by the Assistant Secretary for Enforcement and Operations, US Treasury Department, Mr. Eugene Rossides.

L-R: Kathryn Clark out of frame; Holly Hufschmidt, Phyllis Shantz, me, Laurie Anderson, Eugene Rossides, Secret Service Director James Rowley.

Oath of Office

I will support and defend the Constitution of the United States against all enemies, foreign and domestic; that I will bear true faith and allegiance to the same; that I take this obligation freely without any mental reservations or purpose of evasion; that I will well and faithfully discharge the duties of the office on which I am about to enter, So help me God.

L-R: Holly Hufschmidt, Laurie Anderson, Phyllis Shantz, Director Rowley, me, Kathryn Clark.

The AP reporters had written their press releases and *Parade* magazine had their photos. News and images of our swearing-in spread across the county like wildfire. My parents watched the ceremony on TV in Florida, where they'd retired. As it turned out, Assistant Special Agent in Charge Ken Thompson worked in the Washington field office and became one of our mentors, along with our new boss, Special Agent in Charge Charles Gittens.

In Maurice Butler's book *Out from the Shadow: The Story of Charles L. Gittens Who Broke the Color Barrier in the United States Secret Service*, Gittens recalled, "We needed female agents in the Secret Service for practical purposes and not only for operational purposes. Not just because they were women, but many of the assignments called for women. There were some assignments that women could do better. For example, there were a lot of people that we protected in addition to the president, like foreign dignitaries . . . I was their first Secret Service boss. My bosses told me that 'since you wanted them, we're assigning all of them to your office.' . . . I started as the first African American in the Secret Service, and I could probably understand what they had to go through and how they felt. . . I didn't treat the women agents any differently than the men. They could come in dead tired from an overseas assignment and would be sent straight out on another assignment on the street. They were just as tough as men agents and extremely intelligent."

That day, five of us started our full-fledged journey into the elite and little-known world of the Secret Service. We had been introduced to protective duty, but now we would have the opportunity to experience the rest of the duties and responsibilities of the Secret Service: violations of laws relating to counterfeiting of money and obligations backed by the US government, such as Social Security checks. Not only did we not know what to expect, the men did not know what to expect, either, or how to use us effectively. It was a process of trial and error on both sides. If any of us women were uncertain, or insecure, we masked our true feelings with courage and self-confidence. I was no different. Once we'd been sworn in, I put on my shades and stood before a crowd in full view, my gun, handcuffs, and badge still in the bottom of my purse, ready to protect and serve, and to take a bullet for $8755 a year.

Chapter 10:

January 1972: From Russia, with Love—KGB Agents Flirt with Me

"You hold it like this and twist the head," the Russian Minister of Culture Ekaterina Furtseva said through an interpreter.

At the White House, President Nixon's wife, Pat, held a tray of matryoshka dolls. She watched as Furtseva showed her how one brightly painted wooden doll came apart to reveal another, smaller one. Mrs. Furtseva's face lit up with a child's delight as she proudly presented them to Mrs. Nixon as a gift. I stood in the Blue Room, watching as two powerful women acted like they were greeting their long-lost friend. They had met previously when President Nixon was vice president, and he and Pat had traveled to Russia in 1959. The Nixons were planning another trip to Russia in just five months. I wanted to join them more than anything, but I was sure that would never happen. No "girls" were assigned to the presidential detail.

After the greeting ceremony, Mrs. Nixon walked Furtseva out of the White House to the waiting motorcade of cars lined up on the south lawn drive. I took my place in the back of the follow-up car waiting behind the limo. Behind us was a car full of Russian security men— big guys who rarely smiled. The press waited outside the gate, ready to take up the chase when the motorcade turned right on West Executive Avenue and pulled out onto Pennsylvania Avenue. Although I'd been with the detail since she arrived at National Airport, I had yet to be introduced to her. We headed off to an art gallery, where Furtseva was expected at ten to open a Russian art exhibit.

When we arrived at the gallery, I stepped out of the follow-up car and took my place behind Mrs. Furtseva, forming the south side of the diamond formation of four Secret Service agents surrounding her. We were almost to the door when she turned around and looked me in the eye. An interpreter stepped closer, ready to make introductions. I was wearing my Secret Service identification pin, and apparently she had noticed it. She had a twinkle in her startling blue eyes as she extended her well-manicured hand for a firm handshake. "*Dobroye utro*"—good morning—I mumbled, unsure of my pronunciation. It was more difficult than Cambodian. Her smile broadened and she began speaking to me in Russian. I started laughing.

"I'm sorry, but I don't speak Russian," I replied in English.

I waited for the interpreter to tell her what I'd said, but she obviously understood more English than she let on, because she also laughed and said, "OK, OK, OK." The entourage proceeded inside.

The following day we flew to Los Angeles. Leaving the airport, the motorcade drove north on the 405 Freeway to the Wilshire Boulevard exit, and headed for Beverly Hills. The sun was trying desperately to shine through the smog, but that didn't dim the beauty of palm-studded streets and perfectly trimmed hedges, offering privacy to the Spanish-style homes with their red tile roofs. I wondered what the Russian minister of culture was thinking of our country as we turned onto Sunset Boulevard and arrived at the luxurious pink Beverly Hills Hotel and Bungalows. Built in 1912, the hotel had welcomed an all-star cast of the rich and famous—John Wayne, Henry Fonda, Howard Hughes. Now it was welcoming the Russian minister of culture, her staff, KGB agents, State Department officials, and the Secret Service detail. The Los Angeles field office had loaned us some of their agents to secure the premises. Having protected numerous dignitaries there, they were familiar with the hotel and gardens and had already secured her bungalow. I was thankful our traveling detail had the extra help.

With Furtseva tucked in for the evening, I wandered

around the hotel ground. Stopping in the office, I pe-
rused the postcard rack and bought one to mail my parents. By that time, the Secret Service had delivered my
bag to my bungalow, and I escaped there to luxuriate in
peace and quiet before setting the alarm and falling into
bed. I'd logged eighteen hours that day, flying from DC
to Los Angeles, and I feared the next day would be just
as demanding.

Up at six a.m., I washed my hair and ate breakfast at
the hotel's very expensive restaurant. A group of agents
was already sitting around a table when I entered. They
motioned for me to sit with them. I quickly ordered
scrambled eggs, toast, coffee, and milk. The waiter
asked if I wanted bacon, and I said sure. I was so hungry,
I didn't even look at a menu.

"Sue Ann, do you know how much those extra two
strips of bacon are costing you?" the agent sitting next
to me asked.

"No. Why?"

He smiled, and said, "You'll find out when you get
your bill."

The extra bacon cost five dollars (twenty-eight dollars in 2014). Breakfast more than ate up my fifteen-dollar daily traveling allowance. At least I was ready to
start the day with a full stomach and an empty bladder.
One thing I learned early on in the Secret Service: go to
the bathroom when you can, and eat when you can, because you never know when you're going to get another
chance. (Unfortunately, the "eat when you can" rule has
stuck with me.)

That day we visited the Los Angeles County Museum

of Art and several other art galleries. Everyone babbled excitedly in Russian. At one point, Furtseva grabbed my hand and started talking to me ever so slowly in Russian as we walked among the paintings . . . like *that* would make a difference. I smiled, shrugged, and shook my head to indicate I didn't understand what she was saying. We both laughed. When we finally left the last art gallery, we headed south on Interstate 5 to Disneyland. Because of its size and popularity, there was no way to actually secure Disneyland. We couldn't exactly cordon off the crowds. Instead, we again formed a tight diamond formation around Mrs. Furtseva with two agents on either side of her, one in front, and me behind her. Fortunately for us, the crowds were light that day and the lead agent had no trouble following the Disneyland representative. Mrs. Furtseva's head swiveled around ecstatically, as she took in the sights and sounds of Main Street USA. Much to our relief, she declined to go on any rides.

Walking down through New Orleans Square, we reached a nondescript doorway marked only by a small mirror on the right side. The numbers *33* were etched on the mirror. The local Secret Service agent inserted a membership card in the card slot and unlocked the door.

We entered a beautiful Victorian-decorated foyer and were greeted by our host, who led Mrs. Furtseva and a few others to a French lift. While the elevator took her to the second floor, the rest of us scurried up the stairs and waited for her as the door opened. A maître d' led us into a dining room where we were seated for lunch. Everything about the gorgeous space—from the heavy gold-and-blue fabric-draped windows to the chandeliers—made me think I was in France. The service and the food were immaculate, though not everyone knew how to behave themselves.

As we finished our appetizers, I noticed the detail leader seated next me was scowling. "Look at that State Department guy. He doesn't even know how to hold a wine glass correctly."

"What do you mean?" I asked. I knew little about formal dining etiquette, and even less about wine.

"You don't wrap your hand around the whole glass. You hold it by the stem." When I looked over to the man in question, I saw it was true. His huge, meaty hand was gripping the glass like a baseball bat.

"He should know that," the agent snorted. "The State Department is all about protocol."

I nodded and went back to my meal. The tone of his comment wasn't new to me. I often witnessed tension between various Secret Service agents and the State Department. Politics and security didn't always mix.

The next day the entourage flew to San Francisco. I was sent to the Fairmont Hotel to help secure Mrs. Furtseva's suite, while she and her detail toured Stanford University. The Fairmont Hotel, high atop Nob Hill, offers a panoramic view of the city and the San Francisco Bay. It's also home to the Venetian Room, most famous as the place in which Tony Bennett first sang "I Left My Heart in San Francisco."

When I arrived, the hallway was buzzing with activity as technical protective support staff worked with the physical security of the suite, and telecommunications specialists were working in the suite and the command post room, two doors away. I approached an agent and introduced myself, explaining I'd been sent to help secure Mrs. Furtseva's suite.

"Great," he said. "You're just in time. Go in and do everything Mrs. Furtseva might do—turn the lights on and off, run the water in the bathroom, sit on the toilet, run the shower, things like that."

I wasn't sure I'd heard him right. "Sit on the toilet? Are you serious?"

"You might want to check for plastic explosives before you sit down." He grinned.

OK, I thought. I'd signed up to take a bullet if I had to, but no one had mentioned the possibility of being blown up on my ass. I approached the bathroom, carefully looking around, and reached for the light switch. With one finger, I flipped it up. Whew! Next, I ran water from the hot and cold faucets. OK. I reached in the shower and turned the water on and off. The hot water was hot and the cold water was cold. Good. Then I lifted up the toilet seat and looked under it—nothing. I lifted the top off the tank and looked inside. No red flags. Then I slowly lowered myself onto the toilet seat. What a way *to go* if there'd been anything fishy about it.

When I was done with my part of securing the suite, I took my turn standing guard at the door. Not actually traveling with the person you're protecting, but rather standing a post somewhere, is excruciatingly boring. I used to think that a gorilla standing guard would be just as effective as an agent. If assassins came around a corner and started shooting, the gunfire would alert the other agents, but I would never have had the time to dig my gun out of my purse. The fact is that any agent standing in front of a door deters all but the most determined persons. Besides, assassins normally wait until their target is out in the open to strike.

Mrs. Furtseva returned to the suite to rest before her evening cocktail party. As I stood guard, her KGB agents addressed me in their broken English.

"You very pretty," smiled the tall, good-looking one.

I gave him a slight smile back, trying to look professional, and said, "Thank you."

He grabbed my left hand to look at my ring finger. "Married?"

"No," I replied. "No time."

"Come to Russia with me then."

I gently took my hand out of his and said, "Thank you, no. I like it here. I like my job, too."

He shrugged, pouted, and walked away. It was the first time a Communist KGB agent had wooed me. As a child of the Cold War, I'd been taught that Communists were the enemy. When, in grade school, we'd practiced diving under our desks in response to an air raid blast, I'd pictured Communists with horns growing out of their heads. The fact that it was part of my job to make polite conversation with them—no horns in sight—still felt a little unreal.

That evening, Mrs. Furtseva attended a cocktail party at a private penthouse. It was a small, intimate affair. Thankfully, I didn't have to stand guard outside. Instead, I accompanied her into the party and mingled.

I stationed myself at the edge of the room where I could keep an eye on everyone. We'd done a background check on the host and the guests, but in those days we didn't use magnetometers to screen people for guns.

Out of the corner of my eye, I noticed a woman walking toward me. She took a seat beside me and said, "Lovely party, isn't it? Do you know if that's Mrs. Furtseva over there in the black dress?"

When I turned to reply, I found myself staring at a round-faced, twinkly eyed Shirley Temple. It was a little startling to see the forty-three-year-old adult version of the child star whose movies I'd grown up watching. I adored her.

"Yes, it is. Haven't you been introduced to her yet?"

"No. I've been here a half hour, and I'm sure she knows I'm here. I think she's choosing to ignore me. I'll give her another twenty minutes. If she doesn't want to meet me, I'm leaving. It's been a long day, and I don't need this."

I smiled. "Believe me, I understand about long days."

"You're with the Secret Service, aren't you?" she asked.

"Yes, I'm Agent Sue Ann Baker. It's very nice to meet you."

"Oh, I always wanted to go into law enforcement. I wanted to be an FBI agent or a CIA agent. But they didn't have women agents when I was young."

"Well, I'm one of the first five women they made agents just last month."

"Congratulations. It must be exciting and challenging. Where do you carry your gun?"

I lifted my purse and tapped the side. "You wouldn't believe how heavy it is."

"A few years ago, I worked as a representative to the UN General Assembly. The bag I had to carry was huge and always full of paperwork. All day I carted that bag from one place to another. It was so heavy it actually broke a few veins in my shoulder. I sure don't miss that part of the job."

As we chatted, I realized she was as much in awe of me as I was of her. Finally, Mrs. Furtseva came over. We both stood, and I stepped aside as the introductions were made. In retrospect, that meeting must have paved the way for Shirley Temple to travel to Russia the following September. In 1972, Nixon had appointed her as a representative on the Joint Committee for the US-USSR environmental cooperation treaty. It was during that visit that she noticed a burning sensation in her breast, which led to a breast cancer diagnosis and mastectomy. Her openness about it, at a time when other movie stars and influential women didn't discuss cancer or other health-related issues, is credited with savings the lives of many women.

Mrs. Furtseva left for Russia the next day. I finally had time to write the postcard to my parents:

I'm working many hours—eighteen yesterday, eleven today, but am seeing a lot of museums and art galleries. Flying out of San Fran ten pm and arrive NYC at six am.

Love, Sue Ann

My life was anything but boring. There is no "routine" in an agent's life. Agents in large cities such as DC have to carry both of the agency's loads—protection and investigations—sometimes in the same day. I did what I was told and worked hard to earn the male agents' respect, and to show them I could pull my weight as well as any male agent. I wondered what it would take to accomplish that.

Chapter 11:

February 1972: Finally—
Treasury and US Secret
Service School

The blood seemed to freeze as quickly as it oozed out of my right hand. When we'd arrived at the range that morning, the thermometer had topped out at twenty-eight degrees. Now, snow pelted our faces. It was almost impossible to keep my gloves off. However, with them on, I couldn't use my speed loader to reload my .357 Magnum with an extra six rounds.

What's worse, when I'd focused on the life-size target and pulled the trigger, the hammer had kicked back and bit into my flesh. I hadn't had a strong enough grip.

It was hard with stiff, freezing fingers. The other agents were just as cold and several of them were whining. We all just wanted to retreat to the nearby wooden shack at the National Arboretum, eat lunch, have a cup of coffee, and warm up. We'd qualified, obtaining passing scores in firearms marksmanship with our handguns. Next on the list: the Israeli Uzi submachine gun.

The Uzi could fire up to six hundred rounds a minute, even though a clip didn't hold that many. The instructor explained that it was normally fired in short bursts, but when it was put in full automatic, it would float up and to the right across the black paper silhouette of a body. In one sense, it was exhilarating; in another sense, I was discouraged that I couldn't hold it in one place. It was a great weapon because it was small with a folding stock, and lightweight. Agents could easily hide it from the public under their trench coats when walking in a parade, for instance. It also fit nicely in an agent's briefcase. In videos showing John Hinckley's attempt to assassinate President Reagan in 1981, it can been seen in an agent's hands, pointing upward, but ready to take on multiple attackers. The Secret Service used the Uzi from the 1960s to the early 1990s, when it was replaced by Heckler & Koch MP5s and FN P90s.

As we prepared to wrap up a frigid training session, I ducked into the bathroom, slipped a Kotex under my coat, and carefully wedged it beneath the shoulder of my sweater. When I'd shot the .12 gauge shotgun with slugs before, the sharp recoil had nearly brought me to tears. I don't know which of us five women dreamed up this defensive measure, but I'm sure it wasn't one of the guys. I came out of the bathroom, stepped up to my position, held the shotgun tight into my shoulder, and squeezed the trigger. BAM! I smiled to myself. It wasn't so bad this time. Some of the male agents around me winced as the shotgun slammed into their shoulders, but I kept my secret to myself and made it through another qualifying round.

I'd been to the indoor and outdoor shooting ranges several times, but it wasn't until February 1972 that I attended Treasury Law Enforcement Officer Training School No. 680. The school entailed 244 hours, or six weeks of classroom and hands-on experience. Any investigative cases we had been working had to wait, and for once, we couldn't be used for protective assignments. This was a full-time school. Agents from other federal agencies that were under the umbrella of the Treasury Department attended school with us: Bureau of Alcohol, Tobacco, and Firearms; US Customs; and Bureau of Narcotics and Dangerous Drugs. Laurie Anderson and I were the only female agents in the class with fifty-eight males. We were taught basic criminal investigative techniques along with federal court procedures, conspiracy laws, and rules of evidence. We learned how to search people, cars, and homes, and how to collect and preserve evidence. Men and women searching each other made for some amusing comments, especially when male agents were patting us down and got to yell, "Spread them," as they kicked our legs apart. I took a lot of good-natured kidding.

I also had to prove my marksmanship, along with fingerprinting, interviewing techniques, surveillance, and photography. The legal aspects that I had to learn for the job seemed overwhelming at times. In the end, I felt like I should have gone back to school, picked up a few more courses, and gotten my law degree.

TREASURY LAW ENFORCEMENT SCHOOL NO.680
ENFORCEMENT LAW AND CRIMINAL INVESTIGATION
FEBRUARY 1 – MARCH 16, 1972
THE DEPARTMENT OF THE TREASURY
WASHINGTON, D.C.

When Treasury school finished, agents returned to their respective agencies for more training. While waiting for my next school session to begin, I worked six weeks in the DC field office doing background investigations for top-secret clearances on applicants applying for employment with the Secret Service and other federal agencies. By the end of April, I was off to Secret Service Special Agent Training with thirty-three male agents and Kathy Clark. While all federal agents get a good overview of law and procedures in Treasury School, they drill down to the specific laws of their agencies in specialized training. For instance, only Secret

Service agents are trained on detection and manufacturing of counterfeit money, and protection of dignitaries, while the Bureau of Narcotics and Dangerous Drugs (now the Drug Enforcement Agency, or DEA) would be trained in the illegal manufacture and distribution of narcotics.

During the first part of my schooling, I learned the fascinating history of the Secret Service. In 1850, Pinkerton's National Detective Agency was formed, which worked with law enforcement to solve crimes throughout the United States. During the Civil War, Pinkerton served as head of the Union Intelligence Service, which was the forerunner of the US Secret Service. Up until 1861, hundreds of banks were allowed to print money under state charters, resulting in thousands of varieties of paper currency. When the National Bank Act was passed in 1864, it still allowed thousands of banks to issue national bank notes, but they had to have the same design. Because no one central bank issued currency, by the end of the Civil War, counterfeiting was rampant. The Secret Service was then formed, and its sole mission was to stop US currency counterfeiting. Two years later, they were also charged with "detecting persons perpetrating frauds against the government." This opened up investigations into the Ku Klux Klan, smuggling, mail theft, and land fraud. It wasn't until 1901 that Congress requested presidential protection after the assassination of President William McKinley. By 1908, President Roosevelt transferred a handful of Secret Service agents to the Department of Justice, which formed the beginning of the FBI. The Secret Service's responsibilities continued to grow over the years, as they protected more and more people and investigated more and more crimes. By 1971, the agency was protecting the president, the vice president, their immediate families, former presidents and their spouses, major presidential and vice presidential candidates and nominees, diplomatic missions in the DC area, and visiting heads of foreign governments or anyone else the president directed the agency to protect.

Secret Service Special Agent Training School Class

It was an exciting day when my class boarded a chartered plane and flew to the Crane & Co. paper mill in Massachusetts to learn how the special US currency paper was made. I remember the mill stunk like dead rodents. As I looked down into a vat of pulp stirred by metal arms, a man dumped in a bucket of red and blue fibers. That was one of the main security features of our currency. The fibers could literally be pulled off the paper surface. Counterfeiters could only print threads on high-quality paper. If you couldn't actually pull them out of the paper, the bill was counterfeit.

Back in the classroom, we learned how to detect counterfeit money, peering through microscopes to recognize raised intaglio printing on different parts of a bill. We were given tests to identify counterfeit bills. Some were easy to recognize, but others were not. It all depended on the craftsmanship of the counterfeiter. Forty-four years later, counterfeiters and *funny money* still exist.

According to the Secret Service Annual 2013 Report, they recovered approximately $156 million in counterfeit US currency; arrested 2,668 criminals as a result of counterfeit investigations; and suppressed 262 counterfeit manufacturing plants. Since 1986, they have recovered approximately $630 million in South American-produced counterfeit US currency that was passed and seized globally. The Civil War may be over, but the legacy of counterfeiting is not.

My class also viewed the Zapruder film and the Orville Nix film, both of which showed the assassination of President John Kennedy frame by frame. The horrific image of the president being shot bore into our minds a great sense of responsibility, and it reminded us that an attack could happen in the blink of an eye. Is this how I was going to make my life count? I wondered. It was then that I internalized the reality I could be shot saving someone. A chill ran through me. The room was quiet, except for the hum of the projector as it showed Agent Clint Hill sprint from the follow-up car to the limo. After her husband was shot, Mrs. Kennedy climbed out of her seat onto the back of the limo, reaching for her husband's brain matter. Agent Hill got her back into the seat and rode on the back of the car to the hospital, shielding her from any other bullets. His years of training and mental preparedness kicked in exactly when they were needed. No one could have done it better or faster, and we all knew that if the time came on our watch, hopefully we would do the same thing.

Being a Secret Service agent meant taking a bullet for the people we protected. Our other responsibilities notwithstanding, this was the most fundamental aspect of our job. I was trained not to duck during an assassination attempt. Instead, I was trained to defy all common sense and place myself in harm's way if it meant saving the life of a protectee. We trained for it during mock assassination attempts, so that muscle memory would take over in an emergency situation. It wasn't a matter of thinking—just acting.

I took another field trip with the class, this time to Andrews Air Force Base to tour SAM 27000, the president's plane. It is only called Air Force One when the president is on it. The Boeing 707 was customized from nose to tail with the president's office just inside the door, carpeted flooring, leather chairs, comfortable couches, a medical office, a dining room, conference table, and guest quarters. There were also cute little plastic cigarette packs everywhere with the presidential Seal embossed on them and, of course, White House matches to go with them. Each agent received one as a souvenir. SAM 27000 served until 2001 when it was decommissioned and subsequently put on display in the

Ronald Reagan Library in Simi Valley, California.

Of all the training I received, it was the physical fitness evaluation that nearly did me in. There were no standards for women, so no one was sure if we should be expected to be able to do the same things as the men or not. I was expected to run a mile, which I barely could do—thanks to smoking. I couldn't do a chin-up to save my life, but I was great at sit-ups. In a hand-to-hand combat course, we were taught come-along holds to control prisoners and takedown moves for assailants. That was fun and easy even against the big guys, but it was a far cry from the judo and karate some newspapers said we were versed in. Today there are standards, and they are different for men and women, mainly in upper-body strength and how many chin-ups are expected. If they had been in place in 1972, I am not sure I could have passed them. On the other hand, I probably would have risen to the occasion and bulked up. No excuses. Wonder Woman would have done it!

As chilly spring days grew warmer, I started to get tired of being in a dark classroom for days on end. As luck would have it, one day our instructor announced, "Tomorrow, come dressed in comfortable shoes and clothes you won't mind getting dirty." Everyone was curious. What would we be doing?

The next day, dressed in sweatpants and a T-shirt, I arrived at training just as the sun was coming over the horizon. There was an excited buzz in the air. The instructor announced that we'd be learning how to jump into and out of a four-door sedan—while it was moving. I don't think they drove more than about eight to ten miles an hour, but it was obvious I'd better not miss my step. The instructor demonstrated it twice for us, once while the car was stationary and once while it was moving. I watched intently, because I sure didn't want to wipe the pavement with my face and hurt my body or my pride. When it was my turn, I scooted toward the door, I turned so my butt was on the edge of the seat, and I held the door open. I looked down at the asphalt flying by. My heart was pumping in my ears. When I was ready to make my move, I half-stood and propelled myself out of the car. My feet hit the pavement running. Success! To get back into the moving sedan was worse, in some ways. Basically, I ran along beside the car, opened the door, and timed it to dive headlong into the back seat. By the time I finished with that exercise, I was hot and winded, but unscathed.

Jumping on and off a limo fitted with wide running boards was easier. The car we used was a replica of a limousine in which the president might be riding. I practiced walking beside the car with my hand on it until the car sped up, at which point I jumped on the running board and held onto the grab bars. When the car slowed, I jumped off, making sure my feet were moving as fast as the car. Excitement rippled through me as I jogged alongside the limo that day. I could actually imagine doing this with a protectee in the vehicle. I finally knew I was a real Secret Service agent, and it was a huge relief to feel, for the first time, like I knew what I was doing. When the class ended, we received our certificates of completion and headed back to our respective field offices. I returned to my DC office desk, more confident and ready to tackle anything they threw at me. Well, almost anything . . .

Secret Service Special Agent Technical Security School Class

Chapter 12:

March 1972: High Fences, Short Skirts, Muddy Trails, and Back Alleys

My government steel-gray metal desk was pushed against a wall in a bullpen area at the Washington field office (WFO). No one got a special office unless they were the special agent in charge (SAIC), or the assistant special agent in charge (ASAIC). Most of the time, the bullpen was just about empty. Few agents worked at their desks. They were either out in the field investigating cases or on a protective assignment. I could be catching up on paperwork, or making phone calls, only to be told to go to the Sheraton Hotel and stand post because the president had decided to have a luncheon meeting there. The job required a lot of adaptability.

The squad I was assigned to fell under the "detecting fraud against the US government." That included investigating theft of any obligations backed by the US government such as Social Security checks that were stolen, forged, and cashed.

I opened a file folder from the huge stack on my desk. In each folder was a different check forgery case. While I'd been traveling and attending school, my cases must have bred at night, because they'd multiplied in my absence.

"What am I supposed to do with this?" I asked my supervisor as I stood at his office door, waving a supposedly stolen check—signed with an *X*—in the air.

He looked up at me as though the answer were perfectly obvious. "Who's the complainant?"

I checked the folder. "Someone named Dale Benham."

"Where does he live?"

"Somewhere in Virginia." I thumbed through the file. "Fredericksburg."

"Great. Drive out to Virginia and interview him. Get handwriting samples. We need to determine if he signed the check and just reported it stolen, or if someone else actually stole it and forged his X."

"Handwriting samples? Are you serious?" I asked incredulously.

"Completely, Sue Ann. Take Phyllis with you. Do you think you two girls can handle this?" he smirked.

I stalked over to Phyllis's office and explained the

assignment.

"Handwriting samples?" She seemed as surprised as I'd been. "What is this? Some kind of prank?"

"Come on, Phyllis. Let's go. I'll drive."

We headed south on I-395 toward Fredericksburg. Two hours later, as a heavy rain battered the highway, we realized we were lost. Phyllis tried to reach the office on the radio, but there was no answer. We must have been out of range. Phyllis opened the AAA map I kept in the glove compartment and tried to figure out where we'd gone wrong.

"OK, we need to go back a couple of miles and turn left instead of right at that stop sign," she suggested.

With Phyllis's adept navigation, we were soon back on track. Before long, we found a rusting mailbox on a tilted post with the address we were looking for, in faded black numbers. A six-foot-high wooden gate with a padlocked chain wrapped around it blocked the entrance. The rain had slowed down to a sprinkle, and we could see the house a hundred yards up the sloping trail.

"Well, hell." I eased the car into the driveway entrance and put it into park. "I guess we're going over the gate."

Phyllis wasn't amused. "And take a mud bath? In a skirt?"

"You go first, Phyllis. If you can make it over in a skirt, anyone can."

She laughed and rolled up her sleeves. "I'm sure glad none of the guys are here to see this."

With her usual can-do attitude, she climbed the gate, swung a leg over, and dropped to the other side. I tossed her my briefcase, grabbed the top of the gate, and followed her. We quickly discovered the mud-covered driveway was thick with cow pies. With each step we took, our shoes made a sucking sound in the mud. Slowly, we slogged our way up to an old farmhouse. Three beat-up cars sat under a naked maple tree. Scrawny black-and-white speckled chickens ran away from us and dodged between the cars. We heard dogs barking, but couldn't see any. Fear swept through me. Were they chained? I was sure we were going to be attacked any second.

"I don't like this," I said. "No one even knows where we are."

"I don't like it either, but we're here, so let's just get it done," replied Phyllis. "We'll never live it down if we go back to the office empty-handed."

Stepping onto the porch, which was littered with Mountain Dew bottles, beer cans, and an old Sears washing machine, we tested the boards before taking each step. This was not a place I wanted to fall through some rotten board and break a leg.

We knocked on the door. After a few long moments, it opened a crack, and an elderly gray-bearded man peered out. His bushy eyebrows hovered above rheumy eyes, and a cloud of cigarette smoke preceded him. His smoke-stained yellow teeth matched his right index and middle finger.

"What do you want? How did you get up here?" he growled.

"Are you Dale Benham?"

"Yeah. Who wants to know?"

"We're with the Secret Service, and we're here concerning the Social Security check you reported missing. I'm Agent Baker and this is Agent Shantz. Our car is parked at the bottom of your hill. We've driven from DC and didn't want to miss the chance to meet you, so we climbed over the gate and walked up here. I hope that's OK. May we come in for a few minutes and ask you some questions, so we can get this cleared up, and get another check issued to you?"

The door opened a little wider. I looked in and saw two middle-aged brawny-looking men in bibbed overhauls sitting at a kitchen table with drinks in their hands and a bottle of bourbon sitting between them. This definitely was not a good situation. The odds were against us three to two. Good thing we had our guns. At first glance, I had no idea *how* drunk they were, or what they might be thinking. The larger of the two men looked directly at me, grinned, and winked, motioning us to come on in. When we walked into the kitchen, the acrid odor of smoke, booze, leftover food, and garbage hit me. Glancing around, I observed dishes piled high in the sink, and a cast-iron skillet on the stove with something that looked like vomit in it. The whole place was filthy. No one got up out of their chairs, so we stood awkwardly.

"Your check has been cashed, sir," Phyllis explained. "When we find the guy who stole it out of your mailbox and cashed it, we'll be able to show that it isn't your signature on the back of the check. We need a sample of your handwriting."

"I can't write," he said.

"We don't need you to write, we just need you to make ten of your *X*'s the way you do when you sign your checks."

He sat down and Phyllis handed him the signature card. Finding a pen, he shakily started writing his *X*'s. The other two men leaned back in their chairs to get a better view of Phyllis in her short skirt. Then suddenly, the larger of the two men leaned forward and scooted his chair back from the table. He made an attempt to stand up, still leering at Phyllis. I opened the flap of my purse and put my hand inside, feeling for my gun as he gave up and settled back into his chair.

"Thank you, sir," Phyllis said as she took the card from Benham's hand. "We'll turn this in to our hand-writing experts. You've been most helpful."

"That's OK. I'd drive you down to the gate, but my car wouldn't make it back up in this mud. I reckon you got up here—you can get back down."

We edged our way to the door. Outside, we were more than happy to slip-slide down a muddy path if it meant moving away from the farmhouse. We were both grateful to be out of there safely.

Once we were back in the car, Phyllis snapped her seatbelt on and said, "Get me back to the DC ghetto where life makes more sense and is less scary."

"Here's hoping that's the last fence I ever climb over!" I complained.

We returned to the office covered in mud, worse for wear and bedraggled by the rain. No one asked where we'd been, what we'd done, or why we'd been gone for five hours. I thought the agents must have had a good laugh while we were gone. Maybe I was overly sensitive, but I always felt that, as a woman, I had to work twice as hard to prove myself. I'm not sure if any of the male agents in their suits and Florsheim shoes would have done what we did. Then again, maybe they wouldn't have felt a need to.

Several days had gone by when a fellow agent, Bud, came rushing into the room. "Sue Ann, are you free? I need someone to go with me for an arrest. I've got an informant who just called and said he was going to be playing some basketball with Jerome."

I was flattered. Bud had been an agent for eight years, and he was asking *me* to go with him to make an arrest? Then I looked around and realized there weren't any other agents in the office except the guy on desk duty to answer phones and a guy in the communications room manning the radio.

"Who's Jerome?" I asked.

"A guy I've wanted for two months. He's head of a check forgery ring the Postal Inspectors and I have been working in southeast DC. Right now we've got him on seven counts of postal theft and forgery of Social Security checks. Maybe this time I'll finally get him."

"I'm in," I said.

We pulled out of the underground garage in a Secret Service car and turned on Nineteenth Street NW.

"I think we need to avoid Seventeenth Street," Bud directed. "It's become a big hole for the whole block where they're digging it up for the Metro they're building. It's a mess."

We crossed the Anacostia River into the southwest quadrant of DC, a predominantly African American area full of drugs and crime. I drove past brick row houses, housing developments, and trash-littered streets, while Bud looked for the address.

"There it is. We just passed Jerome's house. Turn here and drive around the block. Let's see if we can see anyone in the alley." I slowed down as we passed the alley behind his house.

"Damn, there he is playing basketball with all those guys," Bud said excitedly. "Pull over up there and I'll call for backup."

We stuck out like two French vanilla jelly beans among the licorice. Anyone in the neighborhood would have made us for cops.

After I parked, we waited for ten minutes, but no other agents showed up. Bud, afraid Jerome would get away, didn't want to wait any longer.

"Drive up the alley, Sue Ann. We'll just have to arrest him ourselves."

Panic ran through me. I'd never arrested anyone this way. In my past police experiences, I'd always been part of a group of officers or agents when a bust went down. Now we were a group of *two*. I'd also only been in the Anacostia area once before, when I worked in the youth division at MPD. It had not been a good experience. That time I was with another white female officer, and our car had been stoned by a group of men shouting, "Get out of here, you fucking pigs—you with the skinny white legs." I was insulted by the legs remark.

I eased the car carefully into the alley. It was extremely narrow and definitely one-way. Midway down it, a group of men shot baskets in a short, makeshift court lined out by chalk on the asphalt. The odds were certainly stacked against us, probably ten to two. I'd have felt better if we'd had backup. Pulling up alongside the group, I stopped the car and Bud jumped out.

"Hey Jerome, my man, how are ya?"

Bud walked directly toward him and firmly grabbed his arm. He was thin but wiry and a good five inches taller than Bud. "Jerome, you're under arrest for check forgery," Bud said loudly.

I'd gotten out of the car and was standing behind my open door. Just when Bud got handcuffs on one of Jerome's hands, Jerome decided he wasn't going to come peacefully. He resisted arrest, swinging at Bud with his free hand, while Bud tried to hold onto the cuffed one. A thousand things ran through my mind in a split second as adrenaline coursed through me. My partner was in trouble. I ran around the front of the car and grabbed Jerome's loose arm. Together Bud and I slammed Jerome across the hood of the car, and I twisted his arm behind him so Bud could get the cuff on his other hand. His friends just stood there smiling. I guess they thought it was funny to see him get arrested by a girl.

We pushed Jerome into the car just as his girlfriend came running out of the house screaming profanities. She ran across the cement patio and pushed her way through the guys and headed straight for our car.

"Lock the doors and let's get out of here," Bud yelled at me.

I reached back and slammed my hand on the lock, pushing it down, just as the girlfriend grabbed the door handle and tried to open it. I'm not sure, but I think I peeled rubber getting out of that alley. I may have looked composed on the outside, but my insides were quivering like grape jelly.

Back at the office, the story spread like wildfire. What I didn't know was that our backup had arrived on the scene, and pulled into the alley just as we were making the arrest. They couldn't believe what they saw—a girl agent fighting with a perp. I heard a lot of congratulations from other agents over the next couple of days, and it felt good. It was the first time I'd been put to a physical test and I'd passed. Now the agents knew I would step up in a confrontation. *I knew* I would step up.

Chapter 13:

June 1971 to May 1972: I Witnessed History—Tricia's Wedding, Nixon's China Trip, Wallace Assassination Attempt

The morning of Tricia Nixon's wedding, between bursts of pouring rain, White House staff rushed to secure fresh flowers to a grand arbor in the Rose Garden. Meanwhile, I was on the other side of the White House, preparing for the role of a lifetime—as Tricia Nixon.

Had Tricia not planned her wedding outside in the White House Rose Garden—a first—the day, and the ensuing security preparations, would have been much simpler. Instead, her choice of venue forced the White House staff to plan two weddings: one outside and one inside, in case of bad weather. Trusting the meteorologist, however, she held firm to the Rose Garden, which had been decorated in hundreds of yellow and white roses for the occasion. And to her delight and the staff's surprise, late that afternoon, as guests were arriving, the rain stopped and the sun broke through the clouds. Just as Tricia had envisioned, she and Harvard Law student Edward Cox shared their vows in the glorious garden. Afterward, in the East Room, the newlyweds celebrated with a 350-pound cake and dancing.

But unlike other White House galas, this one was not open to the media. True to form, however, the media simply assumed their invite had been lost in the mail.

As the dancing drew to a close, Tricia and Ed prepared to depart, first changing into their travel clothes. I tucked a last pin into my blond updo and checked my reflection in the mirror. Not quite a dead-ringer, but not bad.

"Go around to the south lawn and wait in the limousine," a supervisor instructed me and my partner for this very special operation, a tall, trim agent with light-brown hair.

Show time. After we hustled into the vehicle, the limo driver started the car and slowly pulled out of the south gate. I sat in the back in the curbside seat, my partner beside me, as we drove through the streets of DC, hoping to lure the press to follow us instead of the bridal party. We waved to people on the street and they waved back. No doubt a lot of people went home that evening and told their family they'd seen Tricia Nixon and Ed Cox on their wedding day, but the press was not fooled for a minute. No one followed us, but I had too much fun to care.

The following February, in a torrential downpour, I stood post on the tarmac at Andrews Air Force Base in Maryland guarding the field. Air Force One, motors purring, sat fifty yards from me, waiting for the Nixons to arrive in a helicopter from the White House. It was a big day for President Nixon and the world. He and Mrs. Nixon were heading to the People's Republic of China, to visit Chairman Mao Zedong and Premier Zhou Enlai. It was the first-ever presidential visit to China, and Nixon knew he would always be remembered for it. During the visit, he laid the groundwork to establish trade with China. On television, Americans once again saw images of China, a nation they had not seen in over two decades. The Nixons were toasted at banquets; they toured schools, communes, and hospitals; and they visited the Forbidden City and the Great Wall. The president forged new relationships, and Nixon came home to win the 1972 election in a landslide. He would always say that his trip to China was "the week that changed the world."

After only a few minutes on the tarmac, I was soaked down to my underwear. I stood there for over an hour with no umbrella and tried to shelter my purse and my radio. Even in my waterlogged state, I knew I was witnessing history being made, as I saw the Nixons walk up the ramp to the plane and disappear inside. It was a privilege and an honor to witness the beginning of his historic trip.

Three months later, I was standing in the radio room at the Washington field office when a call came in that we all dreaded. Alabama governor George Wallace had been shot while campaigning in a shopping center in Laurel, Maryland. He was one of the presidential candidates running in 1972, and by law, was protected by a Secret Service detail. As a segregationist from the Deep South, Wallace worried about assassination attempts, as well he should have. This was his third run for the presidency, and he was well known for his segregationist attitudes. In 1963, he'd attempted to block black students from enrolling in the University of Alabama, and had intervened again when four black children attempted to enroll in white elementary schools in Huntsville. During his inaugural speech as governor, he emphatically stated, "Segregation now! Segregation tomorrow! Segregation forever!" Extremely popular among whites in the South—not so much in the North. He usually wore a bulletproof vest while campaigning. On what was an unusually hot, humid May day, however, he did not. After giving his speech from behind a bulletproof podium, he entered a seemingly friendly crowd to shake hands—against Secret Service advice.

Would-be assassin Arthur Bremer was waiting for Wallace with his hand extended, but not for a handshake. He fired his .38 caliber revolver, hitting Wallace four times in his midsection. One bullet lodged in his spinal column and left him paralyzed from the waist down. Another bullet struck Secret Service Agent Nick Zarvos in the throat and lodged in his jaw. (He underwent seven hours of surgery but eventually recovered and returned to work.) Another bullet slammed into Wallace's personal bodyguard; and another hit a woman in the crowd. Bremer was subdued by agents as Wallace lay on the ground, his body protected by his wife, Cornelia.

The mood in the radio room was tense, as agents crowded in to listen as events unfolded. ASAIC Ken Thompson quickly dispatched us.

"Ron, you, Sue Ann, and Ed go out to Laurel," he said. "Team up with an FBI agent and a county police officer and take witness statements. Make sure they're included in the interviews, so we won't have any problems in the future with someone claiming anyone was withholding information."

We climbed into an unmarked car. Ed put a magnetic rotating red gumball light on the roof, and we sped off at 80 mph—down the wrong side of the interstate.

I screamed at Ed, "Slow down. The guy's already shot. Let's make sure *we* get there alive." When he saw oncoming traffic, he drove over the grassy median and got on the right side of the road. He slowed down—but not much.

We arrived at the shopping center and the scene was chaotic. People were being detained until their statements were taken. I interviewed three or four people that afternoon, as did the FBI and a local police officer covering the shooting. We each asked any questions we wanted and made sure we all heard the answers. No one we talked to knew the shooter, and only one person had been close enough to actually see the shooting.

After we'd finished taking statements, I was directed to go to the Holy Cross Hospital in Silver Spring to guard Mrs. Wallace. When I arrived, the place was swarming with news media and well-wishers. I wove my way through the crowd of law-enforcement people to a waiting room. Then I saw her, a beautiful woman with thick, curly, disheveled hair, still dressed in her blood-stained white suit. She was incredibly composed and gracious to me. I felt profoundly sad for her, even though I didn't like her husband's politics.

I waited with her for what felt like ages while her husband was in surgery. All the other agents there were men, and I hoped my presence was a little more comforting. Eventually, I was relieved by another agent, who planted himself outside the waiting-room door. I hugged Mrs. Wallace good-bye and drove slowly home that night, shaken by the shooting.

Wallace survived the shooting, only to be paralyzed from the waist down. He was in constant pain for the rest of his life. He would run one more time for president, and fail. He and Cornelia divorced in 1978. By 1983, he declared he was a born-again Christian and that he had been "rehabilitated" and no longer believed in segregation. He died of heart failure in 1998.

Wallace's attacker, Arthur Bremer, had intended on killing President Nixon, but could not find an opportunity "because of tight security." Instead, he followed Wallace around the country while he campaigned. In a police search of Bremer's car after the assassination attempt, they found a blanket, a pillow, a 9mm four-teen-shot Browning automatic pistol, binoculars, a portable radio with police bands, and photographic equipment. Bremer would eventually be sentenced to sixty-three years in prison—later reduced to fifty-three. He was released in November 2007 after serving only thirty-five years.

In one of life's little ironies, my next protective assignment would be with another political candidate—a woman who happened to be black.

Part III:

The 1972 Presidential Campaign

Chapter 14:

June 1972: Ain't No Joke, Ain't No Jive, Shirley Chisholm Has Arrived

"What a dump! Hey, Joe," I called to another detail agent, "did you see the bucket of sand on the second floor that's supposed to be the fire extinguisher? I can't believe we're staying in this hotel."

"Cool down, Sue Ann," Joe said. "The detail leader is checking on it. You're not the only one who is unhappy."

I peeked out from behind the lobby curtain. "There are prostitutes and freaks in front of the building. What was someone thinking to put us here?"

"The Bossert Hotel is supposed to be the best hotel

131

in Brooklyn."

"Maybe it was in 1909, but it sure isn't now," I snorted.

"Look," Joe said, his patience wearing out, "go get settled in your room, grab a bite to eat, and meet me in the lobby in an hour. We'll take the shift car over to the residence. You'll be working the swing shift this afternoon, from three to eleven."

I looked at my room key: 1228. The top floor. I gulped as the elevator doors opened. I held my breath all the way up. When the doors opened again, I finally exhaled and peered down a shabbily carpeted hallway. The smell of stale smoke assaulted my nose. *OK, Baker, make the best of it*, I thought. My room appeared to be clean, but the bedspread was as thin as onion skin and didn't smell much better. The water pressure was terrible, and the pipes rattled, but I had a newish TV and a nice view of Manhattan and the Statue of Liberty. I didn't unpack, hoping we would be moving the next day.

A little later, I met Joe in the lobby and we drove to a row house about twenty minutes from the hotel, in Bedford-Stuyvesant. Shirley Chisholm was the first black woman to be elected to Congress in 1968, and now she was blazing a trail for other minorities as the first black woman to run for president of the United States. Walking around the side of her building, we entered her backyard, a cement-block patio eighteen by twelve feet wide. Even though there was a maple tree in one corner, a dozen rose bushes, and a white picket fence, it seemed very small to me. I was glad I hadn't grown up in a city.

Her home was easy to secure. We set up our command post in her basement and settled in. Shirley was out campaigning. That day, my job was to rotate around the house every half hour. I stood post in the front of the house on the sidewalk, then sat in the back alley, and then spent a half hour in the command post. As I wrote my parents, *Who said it was a glamorous job being a Secret Service agent?*

The next afternoon, I met Shirley and Conrad Chisholm. They were both incredibly kind and welcoming. She wore her hair in loose curls piled on top of her head in a bouffant. Her overbite created a lisp when she spoke, which had no effect on her speaking ability or confidence. Chisholm was a passionate speaker. On several occasions, I listened to her work an audience into a near frenzy. Although she was a small woman, size seven, she had a big effect. As a women's rights advocate, she seemed pleased to see a female agent guarding her.

"I'd like to give you my new autobiography," she said, handing me a hardcover, "*Unbought and Unbossed.*"

"Thank you, Mrs. Chisholm. I can't wait to read it." It was a true statement, however, I didn't have time to read it for years.

The title of her book had been her campaign slogan. As I traveled the campaign trail with her, it was clear that she was unbossed. She was a strong, independent woman who wanted to change the face of politics. She was a perfect example of an alpha woman. I admired her.

As it turned out, I didn't get my wish to move out of the Bossert Hotel. Instead, I lived there for two months. Today my extended stay on the campaign trail would never happen: Agents protecting presidential candidates work three weeks on, three weeks off. In 1972, however, when you were assigned to a candidate, you were with them right up until the convention or election in November. Working twelve- to sixteen-hour days, seven days a week, for weeks and weeks, with no days off, made for very exhausted agents. There is only so much the adrenal glands can take and still be alert.

Chisholm proved to be an inexhaustible campaigner. On a single May day, she made seven campaign stops throughout New Jersey and New York. During one of those many stops at a private backyard fundraising event, I asked the advance agent to direct me to the bathroom. "Yes, just go inside, through the kitchen, and it's on the right. Go ahead. I've got this covered."

When I reached the bathroom, my worst fears were confirmed: I'd started my period! It was unexpected, and I was not prepared. Panicking, I went through cupboards and drawers looking for anything that would be helpful. I finally found a Kotex, but had nothing with which to secure it. Oh well, it was better than nothing. I felt horrible about invading the hostess's privacy in her bathroom, but I had no choice. It wasn't like I could borrow supplies from my colleagues.

The next day, I flew to DC to help with an advance for a fundraising cocktail party in Arlington. I consulted my checklist: notify the Arlington police that Shirley Chisholm and her Secret Service detail would be in the area the following day; drive the routes that would be taken from the airport to the cocktail party; note the closest hospitals in between; make arrangements to have an agent from the WFO at the airport to work with airport authorities upon her arrival; make arrangements for a limo and two follow-up cars; secure a place for them to park at the terminal; meet with the hosts of the party and walk through their house to survey the premises. She enjoyed a wonderful evening of fund-raising.

That night, I had the delicious pleasure of sleeping in my own bed. Given how much I traveled for work, a night at home was a rarity. My apartment had never looked so good. The sheets were squeaky clean and the water pressure was out of this world.

By the next week, I was watching a lizard run across the path leading to the Chisholms' vacation home in St. Thomas. Built high up on a mountain, this small secluded native house was the perfect getaway from the stress of the campaign trail.

The agents and I were in seventh heaven with the accommodations at Bluebeard's Castle, a landmark resort in the heart of Charlotte Amalie, overlooking the harbor. A two-story stone tower, built at least two centuries before, was a well-known feature of the hotel. Colorful hibiscus lined the pathways, and the soft fragrance of frangipani drifted through my shuttered window. Several of the agents even flew their wives down for five days. I, on the other hand, was hopelessly single. Had I had a boyfriend at the time, he would have joined me there. But my choice of profession intimidated many men, and even those who weren't intimidated found it hard to deal with my work schedule. Boyfriends were few and far between. What I needed was a strong, self-assured man—but I hadn't found him yet.

The respite in the sun was short. We returned to Brooklyn Heights, and Mrs. Chisholm prepared for the stump-speech circuit again. Her first trip after her vacation would be to Harlem. I drove with three other agents to the street corner where she would be speaking, to check out the area. When we were done, we decided to get some breakfast.

We found only one place open at seven a.m. The four of us entered and sat down. We waited . . . and waited. No menus arrived. Finally, the only black agent with us got the owner's attention.

"Could we have some menus, please?"

The owner slowly turned his head toward us. He was coal black with a short Afro sticking out from under his white cap. "I can't serve you. You need to leave."

We all looked at him in disbelief. My stomach involuntarily growled. The black agent asked why.

"I don't serve blacks with whites here. You need to leave now."

"How about if I sit over there?" the black agent said, pointing to another table.

Now the owner was getting more forceful. "No, you came in with them. I won't serve any of you. Now get the hell out of here." Two other men appeared from the kitchen, one with a butcher knife in his hand.

Fear coursed through me like water through a fire hose and puddled in my empty stomach. I was white. I was a woman. I was in Harlem. It didn't matter that I carried a gun and was with three male agents who were also carrying. None of us wanted the situation to escalate. We slowly got up and quietly walked out the door into the sunlight. We went a little ways down the block, looking for another restaurant that was open. Seeing none, we retreated to our car and waited for Chisholm to arrive and give her speech.

The next Sunday morning, I was assigned to drive the follow-up car on a trip from Brooklyn into Manhattan. That was a first! I kept the follow-up car a half a car width over to one side or the other behind the limo and stayed close to it. It was nerve-racking in heavy traffic. I had to block merging traffic and swoop in when we changed lanes. When lights turned yellow, I zoomed through the intersection to keep up. I had to be an aggressive driver—and I loved it. I probably made a lot of drivers angry, but no one got between me and that limo.

As the summer wore on, we circulated between Manhattan, the outer boroughs, and DC. I was thrilled to have a front-row seat to watch how the game of politics was played. I wrote my parents:

Shirley Chisholm is a brilliant speaker and I've decided she's the only honest, sincere, down-to-earth, dedicated politician I've ever met. It's a real pity she won't get too far, but I'm sure she's going to have some effect at the convention. If she had more money and could get more national coverage, there's no doubt in my mind she would be as seriously thought of as Wallace. But then money would come from somewhere, and she wouldn't be "unbought and unbossed."

We flew to Miami for the Democratic Convention in July. Mrs. Chisholm gathered 152 electoral votes for her efforts and was fourth among the delegates, ahead of such notables as former vice president Hubert Humphrey and Representative Wilbur Mills of Arkansas. Several of Chisholm's rivals had dropped out of the race in the spring: Edmund Muskie, a senator from Maine; John Lindsay, the New York mayor; Patsy Mink, a representative from Hawaii and the first Asian American woman to run for president; Eugene McCarthy, a former senator from Minnesota, and others. Chisholm, though, had hung on, in spite of the odds against her. In an interview she gave to *Jet* magazine in February 1972, she stated, "Of my two handicaps, being female put many more obstacles in my path than being black."

She had been endorsed by Reverend Jesse Jackson, Representative Ron Dellums of California (until the convention, when he changed his support to McGovern), and feminist leader Gloria Steinem, whom she met with during the convention. In the end, it did not help. George McGovern captured 1729 delegates, or 57.3% of the available delegates, and was nominated as the Democratic candidate.

After McGovern's nomination, my assignment with Mrs. Chisholm came to an end. When I met with her to say good-bye, she gave me a photograph of herself and signed it. "To: Sue Baker—Always look to conscience for approval—not man! Congresswoman Chisholm." I have always tried to live by those words of wisdom.

Shirley Chisholm

Chapter 15:

August to November 7, 1972: The Rocky Trail that Lead to Nowhere

As the 1972 Democratic Convention came to a close, I was assigned to protect Barbara Eagleton, the wife of the vice presidential nominee, Thomas Eagleton, a senator from Missouri. He was George McGovern's running mate for all of eighteen days, until it was revealed that he suffered from bouts of depression and had received electroshock therapy in the past. Eagleton pulled out of the race, and Sargent Shriver of Maryland, a Kennedy in-law, was named in Eagleton's place.

Ironically, I didn't even last eighteen days with Barbara Eagleton. Two days after I was introduced to her, the detail leader told me to go home. That was fine with me. I was more than tired, and she and I butted heads. Perhaps she didn't like to be told what to do. I hopped on the next plane back to DC and luxuriated in my apartment, cooking my own meals and opening a mound of mail. I was amazed my car even started after sitting idle for weeks.

Barbara Eagleton and me behind her at Democratic Convention.

My break was short-lived, however. Three weeks after the Democratic Convention, I was assigned to protect Mrs. McGovern. By that time, I was pretty sure I knew what to expect. I'd protected enough people and had enough training that I felt prepared. Nothing could have prepared me, however, for going on the national campaign trail with the McGoverns. I was awed, both by the politics and the chaos. What became apparent almost immediately to me was that George McGovern's staff didn't know what to do with Eleanor. Growing up in Woonsocket, South Dakota, she and her twin sister, Ila, helped take care of the family after their mother died when they were twelve. A petite size four, she was barely over five feet tall, with curly light-brown hair, always perfectly styled. With her intelligence and debate skills, she'd won a debate against her husband-to-be, George McGovern, when they were in high school. She loved politics even as a teenager. Eleanor stumped for her husband in his run for Senate in 1962 and helped him win his seat. The 1972 election was a much bigger election with global issues to discuss. She made it perfectly clear she wasn't going to let anyone define her role for her. In her memoir, *Uphill*, she wrote, "There is no question that I was a Presidential candidate's wife who was caught between eras, and the subtle discrimination I felt was a severe introduction to male chauvinism in politics." More often than not, she flew solo. She answered political questions that Richard Nixon's wife, Pat, sidestepped. In an *LA Times* article from January 26, 2007, writer Jocelyn Y. Stewart wrote: "Eleanor's appearance on 'Meet the Press' was apparently the first by a candidate's wife in the show's then-25-year history, she wrote in *Uphill*, and she was so nervous she was nearly sick."

In *Uphill*, Mrs. McGovern also describes touring a foundation-garment factory in New York, where she was presented with "an embarrassingly mountainous red-white-and-blue bra," after which she was reported to have said it had been "a very uplifting experience." I remember the trip to the foundation-garment factory as significantly less humorous. An ancient elevator we'd entered during the tour slowly ground to a halt—in between floors. I realized there were too many people on it, but it was too late. That was my first advance assignment; I kicked myself for not checking the elevator and its capacity. It was a steaming-hot August day outside, and even hotter in the factory. The elevator filled with pheromones as panic crept in. I radioed the agent waiting on the first floor, and two men managed to pry open the elevator doors. The floor was three feet above us. Strong hands reached down and carefully lifted Mrs. McGovern out of the elevator. Relief mixed with humiliation flowed over me. She was safe, but I had failed to adequately prepare for every contingency as an advance agent. I was determined that it would never happen again.

The rest of that day was smooth sailing until we reached our hotel for the night. Another agent opened the limo trunk to get a piece of luggage out, and then couldn't get it to stay closed. He slammed it down again and again, but it wouldn't latch. A few minutes passed, and I finally left them to fix it, and ushered Mrs. McGovern into the hotel. It wasn't my fault, but I wilted further into myself. What else could go wrong? As it turns out, plenty.

Mrs. McGovern's suite was on a top floor of the high-rise hotel. We had just settled her in for the night when the fire alarm went off. It was excruciatingly loud. It rang and rang and rang. Was it a false alarm? No one knew. Though there were other agents there, the decision of whether to get her up and make her walk down twenty flights of stairs, or let her stay in her room, fell to me. I was the advance agent. Minutes wore on as we all tried to find out why it was going off. At last, I learned there'd been a small fire in the hotel kitchen, but it had been extinguished. Finally, the alarm stopped ringing and we all let out a collective breath.

That night, as I sank into the cool sheets of my queen-sized bed for a much-needed five hours of sleep, I wondered what the next day held. Hopefully, it wouldn't be as bad as the one that was ending.

The following two weeks were a whirlwind of ac-tivity and travel. I was sent to Austin, Texas, to advance her stop there for a picnic, a reception, and then a press conference. Agent Denise Ferrenz, the sixth female agent to be hired, worked the picnic. She and I bypassed each other as we rotated shifts, and we rarely worked together. She had the most startling beautiful blue eyes and shoulder-length blond hair, and it all matched her personality. Although she did not come from a police background, she was a quick learner and as determined as the rest of us women to make a difference. As soon as Mrs. McGovern was on the ground, Denise took over with the rest of the detail, and I was off to San Francisco to make advance arrangements for McGovern's visit the next day. It was my third assignment as an advance agent, and I'd only been an agent for nine months. I didn't work alone, though. Agents from the nearest field office were always there to support me and show me the ropes of their city. I couldn't have done it by myself, but in the end, as an advance agent, the responsibility fell on my shoulders to make sure the visit was uneventful and safe.

After San Francisco, I flew ahead to Seattle to make more advance arrangements. She would shake hundreds of hands, smile at the cameras, and field political questions. She was always gracious, no matter how tired she really was. By October 15th, roughly three weeks before the election, it all caught up with her.

Back in DC, I planned to work a four-to-midnight shift but was relieved two hours early. A rare date picked me up and we went out for a quick bite to eat. We arrived back at my apartment about eleven. When we walked in, my phone was ringing.

The detail leader, Skip Williams, told me, "Sue Ann, you have to get to Georgetown University Hospital *now*. Mrs. McGovern has been admitted here, and you need to stand guard outside her room until you're relieved in the morning. How long do you think it will take for you to get here?"

I hesitated. "Uh, I guess I can be there in a half hour."

"Good. I'll have an agent relieve you by eight a.m. See you soon."

I put the phone down and broke the news to my

date. It had been a great—if short—evening, and it was going to be a very long night.

I got to the hospital in twenty minutes and found Mrs. McGovern's room. Two shift agents and Skip stood outside her door. When Skip saw me coming down the hall, he walked toward me and quietly said, "One of the nurses is bringing a chair for you. They also have instructions to tell you if her condition worsens. She was brought here because of extreme abdominal pain, and her stomach is being pumped. Maybe the doctor thinks it's something she ate. I think it's sheer exhaustion. Call me if you need to." He and the other agents left.

I paced the hallway to stay awake. It was exactly twenty-seven steps from her room to the nurses' station. On one trip, a nurse followed me back and opened the door to Mrs. McGovern's room to check on her. Around two thirty, the nurse removed the stomach pump tubing, allowing Mrs. McGovern to talk. After the nurse left, she beckoned to me.

"Come on in, Sue Ann. I didn't know you were here. Have you been here all night?" she asked.

"I came about eleven. I'll be here until morning. Is there anything I can get you?"

"No, I'm OK. Why don't you pull up a chair and sit for a while? I'm so sorry you have to be here with me in the middle of the night. Didn't you work today?" She grimaced and repositioned herself in the bed.

I pulled a chair to the side of her bed. "It's OK. I'll get relieved in the morning."

She gave me a quick little smile. "I'm just so tired. They have me flying all over the place, and then there are all these changes in my schedule when George can't make it somewhere."

I was quiet and just listened. It was the least I could do. She needed someone she could vent to—someone she could trust with her secrets.

Her stay in the hospital was brief. The doctors found nothing wrong other than exhaustion. Two days later, she flew back to her hometown, Woonsocket, South Dakota. I was in Cleveland, Ohio, making advance arrangements for her arrival. She was to join George there the next night for a fund-raising dinner. Although she arrived in Cleveland, she again fell ill, missing the dinner. George went on to Toledo while we stayed in Cleveland and flew back to DC the next day. She'd been campaigning for over a year at this point. The polls weren't delivering good news, but the crowds that gathered to hear the McGoverns speak raised their hopes. George was passionate in his stance against the Vietnam War. However, they were fighting an uphill battle against Nixon's popularity and recent history-making trip to China.

Obviously, resting in the hospital for two or three days was not enough to compensate for what her body had been through. Her doctor ordered her to take a vacation. Her choice was between the Virgin Islands and Easton, Maryland, where the McGoverns had a home on the ocean. I was disappointed when I heard she'd chosen Easton. Who didn't want to go somewhere tropical in chilly October? I packed anyway and went to bed.

At one a.m., the phone rang.

The detail leader, Skip, was on the other end. "Hi, Sue Ann. Did I wake you up?"

"Yes, of course. What do you want?" I answered gruffly.

"Eleanor has decided she'd rather go to St. Thomas, so pack for warm weather. We'll be there for five days. Be at the National Airport by eight a.m. Meet you there." The phone clicked.

I reset my alarm, rolled over, and immediately went back to sleep. Flexibility was my middle name. I had flown over thirteen thousand miles in the previous two and a half weeks, and I'd been home five of those days. I was looking forward to standing post under a palm tree outside the home of Henry Kimelman, George McGovern's campaign finance director.

Denise Ferrenz and I both flew to St. Thomas with Mrs. McGovern. We had been agents for long enough that someone had decided we could work the midnight shift. Denise drew the short straw. She sat on post from dusk to dawn surrounded by bougainvillea, listening to the birds chirp in the darkness. The next day, she'd lounge at the pool, drinking a piña colada, unable to sleep. She clearly remembers the trip: "It was awful!"

Two days after we arrived in St. Thomas, Mrs. Mc-Govern invited three other agents and myself for "a drink" on the Kimelmans' poolside patio. As I was the only one on duty, I stuck to Coke. We had a lively discussion of politics, welfare, crime, prison reform, drug addiction, and abortion. We didn't all agree, but we agreed to disagree. No one got angry. I enjoyed listening to the different perspectives. It reminded me of my childhood, when my father and I would debate a topic and then somehow switch sides in the middle of the debate. I grew up wanting to hear opposing views before making a final decision. It's a practice that has kept me open-minded and fair.

The conversation turned to the motorcycle ride some of us had taken the day before to see the island. Mrs. McGovern jumped at the chance to do that. Her press secretary, Mary Hoyt, shuddered at the possible headlines: "Mrs. McGovern breaks arm while motorcycle riding with Secret Service agent during stay in the Virgin Islands to recuperate from illness."

So much for that adventure.

As Election Day drew near, McGovern was still running behind in the polls, but no one discussed it. The brief vacation in St. Thomas helped get all of us through the next twelve days. At a fundraiser at Madison Square Garden two days after our return, I found myself standing on the stage behind Mrs. McGovern while she spoke, and only a few feet away from Rose Kennedy and Shirley MacLean. The crowd was enormous and buoyed everyone's spirits.

For the next three days, she spoke and shook hands in Hartford and New Haven, Pittsburg, Syracuse, Newark, and New York City. When the campaign landed in Manhattan, George decided, on the spur of the moment, that he wanted to walk down Fifth Avenue at rush hour. We stepped out of the motorcade and immediately surrounded the McGoverns as the crowd pushed forward. I had trouble staying close to Eleanor, and that made me anxious. When a reporter stepped between her and us, that was unacceptable. I raised my elbow and shoved it into his back to move him aside.

The McGoverns and me walking down 5th Avenue in NYC

Late in the day on November 1st, George's staff decided that he was too hoarse to speak in Hibbing, Minnesota, at an important Democratic rally. The campaign
sent Eleanor instead, and chartered a small jet to get us
there on time. In her book, *Uphill*, she remembers only
agent Skip Williams, the detail leader, sitting in the co-
pilot seat, while she and Mary Hoyt sat in the back. For
the record, I was squished in there, too. I know because
I'll never forget that trip.

Sucked into a monstrous winter storm, we decided
to reroute to Chicago's Midway Airport, where we could
then determine—safely—if getting to Hibbing was fea-
sible. It was nighttime—the sky was black around us,
and although our altitude was dropping, we couldn't
see any lights below us. Where the hell was the airport?
I got on my Secret Service radio to contact agents on

the ground—to no avail. I left the radio on and tried to exude a calmness I did not feel.

When we finally broke through the clouds, the tops of skyscrapers were whizzing by our windows. We were way off course and far too close to the ground. The pilot had to pull up and bank sharply to avoid hitting a building. After circling around, the pilot made another landing attempt, this time successfully.

We entered a small waiting room at the airport, and Mary went off to find a telephone to call the McGovern staff. They wanted us to go to Hibbing despite the bad weather. Eleanor writes that she found Mary saying, "I won't take the responsibility, the Secret Service won't take the responsibility, and the pilot *will not fly the plane.*"

Mrs. McGovern and me coming out of a care facility she toured.

We stayed in Chicago that night and flew back to New York City the following day to join up with Senator McGovern. In the next four days, we flew with him to Cincinnati; Battle Creek, Grand Rapids, and Lansing, Michigan; Gary, Indiana; Chicago; Waco and Corpus Christi, Texas; Little Rock; St. Louis; Granite City, Illinois; Clayton, Missouri; and back to New York City.

It was crazy. Thirteen cities in four days. Fortunately, we ate (real meals) and tried to get some sleep while flying in between cities. Often I rode in the press plane that followed McGovern's plane. The news people were so punchy by that point in the campaign season that for fun, they'd take turns rolling film reels down the aisle as the plane took off just to see how far they would go before falling over. Reporter Connie Chung was a master at the roll. When we landed, everyone always cheered, glad they'd made one more landing safely.

Two days before Election Day, at DeWitt Clinton High School in the Bronx, a packed house grew restless, shouting for a very late George McGovern. As usual, the campaign sent Eleanor to stand in for him until he arrived. The auditorium was so full of bodies, condensation formed on the windows. Eleanor stood on stage patiently, engaging the audience for as long as she could. But that wasn't good enough. They wanted George.

When he finally arrived, the crowd went wild. Excited to greet well-wishers, he moved to the edge of the stage and leaned forward to shake hands. Meanwhile, I was stuck behind them. If someone opened fire, there was no way I could have moved between the McGoverns and the assailant in time. Sweat rolled down my face. I opened the flap of my purse and put my hand on my gun. More people pushed forward. It may have been an exciting moment for them, but it was one of my worst nightmares. I kept my eyes glued on the crowd and wondered how much more adrenaline my body had left in reserve for the fight-or-flight response I might need.

The McGoverns at DeWitt Clinton High School with me behind them.

The day before the election, we flew from New York to Wichita. As George made a speech to a waiting crowd at the airport in Kansas, a cold rain soaked the ground. Most people held umbrellas. As agents, we did not. My long leather coat was sodden as I climbed back into the plane. There was no way to dry it out before we landed in Los Angeles later that afternoon. We'd flown all that way for another twenty-minute airport rally. It was about sixty degrees with a breeze, and I was chilled to the bone, standing there in my wet coat.

That was nothing, though, compared to what Sioux Falls, South Dakota, welcomed us with that night. The wind was blowing fifteen to twenty miles an hour, and the thermometer hovered just above freezing. My wet coat started to actually freeze and become stiff. As we climbed into the cars and headed for the Holiday Inn, I took a long look around. At that point, I don't know who was more exhausted—the McGoverns, the Secret Service agents, the staff, or the reporters. If anyone had asked us our thoughts that night, and if we were honest, everyone there would have said they were just ready for it to be over with.

The next day, George McGovern conceded defeat in Mitchell, South Dakota. For all that work, all those speeches, and all those handshakes, he lost the presidential election in a landslide to Richard Nixon, who garnered 60.6% of the popular vote. Even with 18–20-year-olds finally able to vote, voters McGovern had counted on, he lost. McGovern carried only one state plus the District of Columbia. I didn't agree with the McGoverns' politics, but I couldn't help but admire Eleanor's passion, honesty, energy, sense of humor, and loyalty to her husband. She fought hard for what she believed in, and that's all anyone can do.

It was a long, sad plane ride home, but even exhausted, we still managed to smile for a photo. Whenever I'm faced with a difficult situation or task, the words Mrs. McGovern always told herself come to me: "You can do it."

L-R: Denise Ferrenz, Mrs. McGovern, and me on Dakota Queen flying home after the election.

Yes, I can. It had been a very long, grueling summer and fall. I had the weekend and one day off after I returned to DC. The Saturday after the election, I gave a dinner party for five close friends. It was the first time in months I could let my hair down, drink a bottle of wine, and truly enjoy myself without worrying about anything or anyone. I definitely needed a change from protection, but I had no idea how I'd ever get out of DC. And then an agent position opened in LA. Would they ever let a girl out of DC?

Two months later, I received a letter from Eleanor McGovern, dated January 4, 1973:

Dear Sue Ann –

As is usual with me this note is a month or more late. I intended long ago to write you of my appreciation for your help and the joy of having you with us. You are all such out-standing people and a real credit to your service.

I can't find the words to express the gratitude I feel and the great pleasure in having you with us.

I would like soon to have Laurie [Anderson], Denise [Ferrenz], and you over to the house with Margo [Hahn] and Mary [Hoyt]. Would such a frivolous thing be possible? We would love to see you again. Please let me know.

Again, a million thanks and the happiest of New Years,

Eleanor McGovern

Jan 4

Dear Sue Ann —

As is usual with me this note
is a month or more late. I intended
long ago to write you of my
appreciation for your help and
the joy of having you with us.
You are all such outstanding
people and a real credit to
your service.

I can't find the words to
express the gratitude I feel
and the great pleasure in
having you with us.

I would like soon to have

Letter from Mrs. McGovern

Laurie, Denise and you over
to the house with Mary and Marg..
Would such a fabulous thing
be possible? We would love
to see you again. Please let
me know.

Again, a million thanks, and
the happiest of New Year,

Eleanor McGovern

Part IV:

Los Angeles

Chapter 16:

August 1973: My Grueling Night Across the Border

I always thought that counterfeit investigations was one of the most challenging and exciting jobs in the Secret Service. I would get to use my brain, more than my brawn, to investigate, arrest, and prosecute counterfeiters. For the most part, I would usually get to drive home every night and sleep in my own bed. One of the field offices that handled a lot of counterfeiting was Los Angeles. None of the female agents had ever been reassigned to another field office. When I heard that a position was open in Los Angeles, I knocked on Mr. Gittens's door. He had been a gem of a boss—even tempered, fair, always ready to listen, and usually with a big smile on his face. I still was nervous about what I was going to ask him.

"Come on in, Sue Ann. What can I do for you?"

"Well, sir, I heard there's a position open in the LA office. I'd like to know what the process is to request a transfer."

He looked at me for a few seconds and said, "You know, they've never let any of you girls be assigned anywhere but DC."

"I understand that, but I just want to know what's required to put in for a transfer like anyone else."

He leaned forward in his chair smiling. "Are you saying that if they don't allow you to transfer, it would be discrimination?"

Now I was dumbfounded. This was coming from the first African American agent. I took a deep breath and said, "You said it, sir, not me."

"I'll see what I can do." With that, I walked out of his office with a hopeful heart.

Two days later, orders were on my desk to transfer to LA. I was the first female agent to leave the sheltered cocoon of DC, thanks to a boss who understood more than most what it felt like to be in the minority.

My mother flew up from Florida to help me pack my apartment. I worked in the office until the day before I left, and seriously have no idea how I would have done it without her. We climbed into my 1972 bright-red Datsun 240Z and headed west. My mother had never been out west before, and I was anxious to show her the country. However, as I quickly learned, flying around the country was much different than driving across it. She couldn't drive a stick shift any better than I could when I was in Germany. She finally got her courage up and managed to get the car moving, onto the freeway, and into fourth gear. It wasn't long before I glanced over at the speedometer and she was hitting eighty-five, twenty miles over the speed limit.

"Mom, do you know how fast you're going? We're going to get a ticket."

She laughed and slowed down, claiming she didn't realize her speed. I think she was just joyful with the freedom from everyday life. My sports car probably fulfilled a dream for her. We couldn't have been happier flying down the desert roads, stopping to sightsee when we came to the Petrified Forest, the Painted Desert, and the Grand Canyon. Seven days later, we arrived in LA and headed south to Orange County. With the checks that had stacked up in my bank account while I was traveling during the '72 campaign, I managed to scrape together enough money to make a down payment on a condo in Fountain Valley. I became a proud homeowner for the first time at twenty-six. My mother stayed long enough to see the condo and hold my hand through the intimidating process of signing a myriad of paperwork and closing the sale. Life was good. I had a new home in smoggy but beautiful California, and I was ready to tackle the world. Mom flew home, and I waited for the moving van to park in front of my condo and deliver my furniture.

It was an hour-long commute to the Federal Building on Spring Street in downtown LA. Every morning, I'd pull into my favorite drive-thru and order a donut and a freeway coffee to go. This was a small coffee poured into a large cup, which left room for it to slosh around without spilling on the stop-and-start drive to work.

It didn't take long to get settled in at my new office, and my first few months there were as busy as ever. One afternoon, toward the end of the day, Special Agent Tom Burg approached me. "Sue Ann, you're going with Joe and Bud. We just got a tip from an informant who knows where Tommy Rodgers is—in Tijuana. His name is Tyrone and he's a pimp, running three girls. He's going to take you to Rodgers. Take the girls with you, too."

It had been a month and a half since I'd arrested Rodgers, a counterfeit money manufacturer. It was the fourth time he'd been arrested for counterfeiting. A chunky five-foot-seven dude who sported black slicked-back hair and a dagger tattoo on his left upper arm, he wasn't half as impressive as he thought he was. His girlfriend's mother had mortgaged her house for Tommy's fifty-thousand-dollar bail. When he skipped bail and fled to Mexico, the girlfriend, Lula, had run off with him.

"Why do we have to take all of them? Can't we just take Tyrone and leave the girls behind?" I asked.

Agent Burg smiled. "Nice try, Sue Ann, but no. Tyrone always takes his girls with him to Tijuana, so you have to take them, too. He's been down there buying heroin from Rodgers. He claims that Tommy is living on the beach just south of town in his new camper van. Since he bought it with a bad check, the car dealership is looking for him, too."

"I guess that makes sense. Do I get to eat dinner first?" I asked.

"Nope. Go now."

I grabbed my trusty peanut-butter-and-cheese crackers out of my desk drawer and ran down the hall to catch up with Joe and Bud. Another agent joined us. We headed for the Federal Building parking lot and climbed through the windows of two unmarked cars. The parking lot was so small, often there was not enough room to open a car door.

Turning left on Spring Street, we drove down streets known for prostitutes and their pimps. By five thirty, we found Tyrone and his girls standing on the corner of Broadway and Fifth Street. He was skinny but muscular, and stood at an imposing six four. Dark complexioned, he had a wild, unkempt Afro and a face only his mother could love. His close-set eyes reminded me of a rat. I noticed that as we spoke, he often clenched his long-fingered hands into a fist. It didn't take a brain surgeon to realize that it was a well-understood silent signal to his girls to behave and keep their mouth shut. *This is going to be an interesting evening*, I thought.

Stopping at a gas station, Agent Joe gave Tyrone just enough money to fill up his gas tank. Exiting the station, our caravan pulled onto I-5 heading south. We kept Tyrone sandwiched between the two Secret Service cars. In San Diego, we picked up two more agents waiting for us at the border, and another car joined the procession. As we crossed the border, we were joined by five Federales—Mexican Federal Police. The motorcade grew longer. We needed the Federales, because the Secret Service has no jurisdiction in Mexico. If all went as planned, the Federales would arrest Tommy Rodgers when they found him and hand him over to the Secret Service at the border.

Tyrone led us to the address where he usually met Tommy. We parked down the street and let Tyrone and his girls go up to the adobe house with chickens roaming around the front yard. The dust flew up in little clouds as the chickens scratched at the ground looking for something to eat. Trying to put my own hunger aside, I adjusted the binoculars and aimed them at the door. Tyrone and his girls finally stepped out of the house— alone. Apparently, Tommy and Lula weren't there, but they were expected by nine a.m. the next morning for a menudo breakfast.

I was ready for a motel and some sleep, but ever-macho Agent Joe, who was leading the search, wanted to show off and make an arrest ASAP. I squinted my eyes and pursed my lips at his pronouncement, but said nothing. Who was I to butt heads with the lead agent? From midnight to two a.m., the whole motorcade drove around to the three or four campgrounds where Tyrone said Tommy had stayed before. We never found his van.

By this time, even the Mexican police were hungry. It was late, but they didn't hesitate to force a small restaurant owner to open his kitchen and start cooking. I ordered a cold beer. I figured the alcohol would kill any bacteria in what looked like hog slop on my plate. Sullen, I poked at my food and kept quiet. The Federales, the agents, and our informants all seemed to be enjoying their food, but I felt more than a little uncomfortable in the smoke- and testosterone-filled room. The Federales laughed loudly, leaning back in their chairs with smirks on their unshaven faces. They glanced my way far too often. I was not in Painesville, Ohio, anymore.

By three a.m., we'd ditched the pimp and his girls for a while, leaving them to sleep in their car in a hotel parking lot in Ensenada. Agent Joe told Tyrone, "You'd better be here when we come back at seven, or the Federales will find you and I won't know who you are."

With that, we spent the next two hours driving around the less scenic parts of Tijuana and Ensenada, looking for Tommy. At daybreak, we found a decent restaurant in which to eat breakfast. I was thrilled I could actually recognize what I was eating. The hog slop had morphed in something resembling scrambled eggs, beans and rice, and a corn tortilla.

Around seven thirty, we swung by the hotel and got Tyrone and his girls. Apparently, there had been a misunderstanding during the night. One of the girl's eyes was starting to swell and turn varying shades of black and purple.

"I got bit by a bug," she explained as she headed into the hotel to wash her face in the restroom.

"We'll catch up with you a little later," Tyrone told Agent Joe.

"OK, but hurry up. We want to get there early and sit on the house before Tommy gets there at nine."

Tyrone made a big mistake by not following us. Tyrone wanted to find Tommy himself—maybe even warn him. We never quite knew. We later learned that as Tyrone entered a campground fifteen miles south of Tijuana, his car's brakes gave out. It rolled downhill, over the lawn, bounced off a small tree, and crashed into a picnic table before coming to a stop. The campground owner called the local police, and Tyrone and his girls were all thrown in jail.

Back in Tijuana, we were fed up with Tyrone. We didn't know where he was and decided we weren't going to wait any longer. The Federales led the way down the narrow streets, back to the house where we hoped to find Tommy. In the early morning sun, an occasional rooster crowed, and the chickens were waking up for another day of scratching in the dirt. After setting up surveillance, we only had to wait an hour. Tommy and Lula drove up, parked, and went into the house. Quietly, the Federales rolled up to the driveway blocking Tommy's van, and charged through the front door with guns drawn. There sat Tommy eating breakfast, spoon in midair. The panicked look on his face melted into submission.

"You know the drill, Tommy. Hands behind your back. You too, darling." Joe cuffed him while I cuffed Lula. We would have read them their rights, but they didn't have any rights in Mexico. I put my right hand between Lula's cuffs, ready to twist them if my prisoner didn't cooperate. I steered her out of the house, past the scrawny chickens, and to a waiting Federale's car.

The motorcade proceeded to the border, where the prisoners were safely transferred into a Secret Service car. The agents showed their appreciation to the Mexican police by letting them keep the brand-new purple camper van. After all, it was in their country. Tommy's face dropped when he realized what was happening. Handcuffed in the back of the agents' car, there was nothing he could do. Agent Joe laughed, "Don't worry, Tommy. The van will be waiting for you if you decide to come back to get it."

I breathed a sigh of relief as we rolled onto I-5 heading north back to LA. The end of a very long night was only one hundred and forty miles away. I wanted a shower, some good food, and a clean bed. The radio squawked. Agent Joe turned up the volume. The San Diego agent said, "I just got a phone call from the Mexican police. They've got two American girls and a black dude locked up in their jail who want our help."

Agent Joe rolled his eyes, "Give them two hundred bucks. That's what we agreed to pay them for helping us catch Tommy. Between the car repairs, towing charges, fines, and damage to the park, that'll probably come pretty close. The girls will figure out a way to make up the difference. Over."

I couldn't help but laugh, an exhausted glad-it's-over-with kind of laugh. I'd seen enough of Mexico to last my whole lifetime. Collapsing into my bed at two in the afternoon, I tallied up my pay as I faded into unconsciousness. On top of my regular salary, I would receive a fifteen-dollar per diem travel allowance and sixteen hours of compensatory time, which I could use when I wanted to take a couple of days off—if I ever could.

Chapter 17:

October 1973: Guns, Pesos, Dildos, and Porn

I stood in the harsh winter sun on an LA street, staring into the trunk of an early model battered white Ford Aurora full of coffee cans and cardboard boxes. The vehicle's owner, a tall, sandy-haired white guy named Rodney, opened up a large box and showed me a stack of one hundred dollar bills.

"These are just for fun," Rodney said. "They're bigger than regular bills."

"Do you make these?" I asked.

"No, I just know the guy who does."

"Can he make them smaller? Like real bills?" I asked.

"Oh, I don't know. I can ask." He reached for a coffee can and popped the lid. "Here's something you might like. I get Mexican pesos and centavos and squash them out a little so they're the same size as quarters. Then I spray them with silver paint. You can use them in vending machines—no problem."

"Really? That's great. What do you sell them for?"

"A roll of forty will cost you only five dollars," he said smiling.

"Here you go," I said extending a five-dollar bill to him. "I'll take a roll." He grabbed the five and handed me a roll. I hoped my partner in the surveillance van was paying attention and that his camera was functioning.

The case had started in late October when an informant, Leroy, told me he knew a guy who sold large reproductions of bills, fake quarters, and porn. In 1973, it was illegal to reproduce currency, no matter what size it was. Twenty years later, the law changed to allow reproductions if they were significantly larger or smaller than a lawful bill and printed on only one side. Even though Rodney's bills were noticeably larger than regular ones, at that time, he was still breaking the law (though the case would hardly be a prosecutor's dream). More interesting to me, though, was whether he would produce authentic-looking counterfeits and try to pass them off as real.

I had partnered with agent Glen Winn on the case. He was one of the good guys, respectful of me as a woman and as an agent. We had a great time working together, and his sense of humor cracked me up.

Working undercover waiting to meet Rodney.

We had set up an initial meeting in a suburban neighborhood, and Glen had parked the surveillance van a
half block away. It had been my first solo undercover
assignment. I sat on the curb while Leroy worked on his
car. When Rodney finally drove up and parked in front
of us, he was wearing sunglasses and struck me as very
effeminate—harmless enough. I put on my shades as he
got out of his car. Leroy introduced me.

After buying the roll of Mexican coins, I pointed to
some larger boxes tucked farther back in the trunk.
"What's in there?" I asked.

"If you're interested, I've got some 8 mm pornos for
sale. They're in color. I could let them go for ten bucks
a reel."

I laughed. "*I'm* not interested in them, but a guy I
know from the bar where I work probably would be. I'll

give him a call. If he's interested, we could meet you tomorrow night."

"Sounds good," he said.

"Can I get a phone number where I can reach you? I'll let you know if my friend is interested in the movies."

"Sure." He opened the passenger door and reached in to open the glove compartment. My eyes were glued on him as he reached in, hopefully only to find a pen. Finally, he came across a scrap of paper and a pencil. He wrote down his telephone number and handed it to me.

After he got in his car and drove away, I thanked Leroy for the introduction.

"No problem," he said. "The guy is a scum bag."

"Well, you're out of it now. I'll bring in another agent tomorrow. Thanks again." I walked over to the surveillance van and tapped on the door. Glen opened it with a big smile on his face.

"Good job, Susie-Q. I think I got some great pictures. We'll know when I get the film developed."

The next evening, I introduced Glen to Rodney as my co-worker. I told Rodney that Glen was potentially interested in buying lots of movies. Glen played his part to the hilt, convincing Rodney that he needed twenty-four hours to view the films and make sure the quality was good. Rodney promptly handed over five of them: *Snow White*, *Tijuana Stag*, *Once Upon a Mattress*, *Life Begins at 40-D*, and *Big John and the Girl Scouts*.

In 1973, defining pornography and whether it was protected under the First Amendment for free speech was a huge debate. Under California's penal code, "every person who knowingly . . . in this state possesses, prepares, publishes, produces, or prints, with intent to distribute or to exhibit to others, any obscene matter is for a first offense guilty of a misdemeanor." In a landmark court decision in 1973, the Supreme Court had ruled that obscene material did not enjoy protection under the First Amendment, but it did establish a three-prong test to define pornography. They rejected the notion that to be obscene the material had to have "utterly no socially redeeming value."

Back at the field office that night, I walked past a closed door and heard hooting laughter from inside. This time, I was not annoyed at being left out. I'd grown used to it. Besides, I knew what they were watching. It was eight o'clock and I was hungry and tired. I headed home, suspecting that the next day would be a long one that would entail obtaining a search warrant and executing it on Rodney's home.

But to my surprise, we didn't bust Rodney the next day. Instead, I was pulled out on a protection assignment and sent to San Francisco. By December, I was working with the FBI in Orange County to catch a fugitive they were after. Two weeks later, at the Secret Service field office, I had to strip search a young female prisoner we'd arrested in a check forgery ring. We fought in a bathroom stall where she tried to flush fake driver licenses she had hidden in the crotch of her panties. I yoked her from behind to pull her out of the stall, but we both fell—on my tailbone on the hard marble floor. I heard the toilet flushing and knew I'd lost the battle to save the evidence. I won the war, however, with my testimony at her trial.

Finally, in February 1974, when Glen and I were both in town, we got around to arresting Rodney. We drove up to his house and saw his car in the driveway. I knocked on the door.

As he opened it, I said, "Hello Rod, remember me and my friend, Glen? He'd like to get some more movies from you. Can we come in?"

Rodney stammered a little, saying the place was a mess, which was an understatement. I'd been in some pretty dirty houses, but this was the first hoarder's house I had ever seen.

"Come on in," Rodney offered.

Glen slowly pushed the door open farther. Rodney backed up and we walked in.

"So do you have any more movies like you showed me? Oh, and some of those hundred-dollar bills like you showed Sue?" Glen questioned.

"Yeah, I do. Let me see how many movies I've got left." He turned to go and get them, giving us time to take in what we could see in plain view. Anything we saw that was obviously contraband, we could seize without a warrant, since he had invited us into his home. When he came back with a box full of films and a pack of large bills, Glen said, "OK, Rodney, my man, we're Secret Service agents, and you're under arrest for alteration of coins and enlarging currency for starters. Turn around."

I thought Rodney was going to wet his pants. I handcuffed him and told him to sit down. After I read him his rights and he declined a lawyer, I asked, "May we search your house?"

"Sure, go ahead. I don't have anything to hide. All I

have is this box of movies and the pack of bills a friend gave me."

He'd apparently forgotten our previous conversations. I looked at Glen and we laughed. It was the beginning of a long night.

After we got Rod seated comfortably—or not—we started poking around in the filth. The more we poked, the more illegal or suspicious things we found. Within a half hour, we decided it was time to call in another two Secret Service agents, the local police department, and the Bureau of Alcohol, Tobacco, and Firearms. We'd found the negatives for the large-currency bills and dies used for altering coins by placing mintmarks on them. We also found one bag of Mexican coins that had been dusted with a "silver substance" under his bed. Fifteen agents and police officers spent over six hours searching the house. We didn't finish searching his home until one a.m. Rod was nervous but polite, and never told us to stop. He finally gave up trying to explain things.

The Long Beach Police evidence report was fourteen pages, single spaced and very thorough. It listed such things as a seventeen-inch color TV and ten Sony and Panasonic tape recorders, all of which had their serial numbers removed. They found numerous uncirculated sets of Canadian and United States Mint proof sets, possibly stolen; plastic bags full of a green leafy material resembling marijuana; multiple bottles of narcotics taken from a hospital; 1737 rolls of pornographic movies and enough evidence to prove he was a distributor of obscene matter; and the cherry on top—a bevy of sex toys that would have made the Marquis de Sade proud.

ATF agents confiscated sixteen one-gallon jugs of distilled spirits for which no taxes had been paid; plus four revolvers and four automatics handguns; one .12 gauge shotgun; and one .30 caliber carbine—all loaded. At that point, my blood started running cold. Eventually, he became a suspect for nine connected murders in the area. Two of the victims worked at the same hospital where he worked as a security guard. I was sure glad Glen had been with me when I'd knocked on Rod's door that afternoon. Maybe Rodney wasn't as wimpy as I thought he was.

To this day, Glen swears he went home that night, stripped outside his back door, and put all his clothes in a large plastic bag. He burned them the next day. His legs were covered in fleabites up to his crotch. I guess they didn't like my skin lotion. Neither one of us knows what became of poor old Rod, but if the news is any indication, he seems to have kept out of trouble for the last forty years—or maybe it's just that he was never caught again.

Chapter 18:

February 1974: Operation Pandora's Box

There are some days that are slower than others. Then again, there's the saying, "When it rains, it pours." This was a wringing-wet week! The day after searching Rodney's flea-infested house, I was in the office by eight a.m. to sort out inventory and start the paperwork for Rod's arraignment in US District Court.

The two other agents who had come to help us the night before had loaded up the company car with evidence relevant to our case and brought it back to the office. Included among these items was a dildo, which quickly found its way into a fellow agent's hands. He taunted me with it, waving the big rubber penis wildly and yelling to everyone within earshot, "Hey, Sue Ann, here's what you need." I was mortified, angry, and disgusted, all at the same time. I don't remember if I said something back or just gave him a digital response.

The incident is not a reflection on the Service, but rather on that particular agent and the hotdog culture of the Los Angeles office. It was a large office and not everyone gave me a hard time, but there definitely was a group of guys who thought they were hot stuff, and who let me know they didn't think I should be there. Recently, I was told by a current female SAIC that if that little incident happened today, the agent would be fired. It was consoling to hear that some things have changed.

The next day, the ASAIC of the office told me about Samuel Byck, a man who'd attempted to hijack a passenger airplane in Baltimore and force the pilots to fly it into the White House. He'd shot a police officer dead at a security checkpoint and pushed his way through the aircraft door, carrying a gasoline bomb and waving his gun at passengers. In the cockpit, he told the pilots to get the plane in the air. When Byck learned the plane was still chocked in place, he shot both the pilot and the co-pilot. Another police officer finally shot and wounded Byck, who then ended his own life by shooting himself in the head. (Sean Penn starred in a movie called *The Assassination of Richard Nixon* released in 2004, in which he played Samuel Byck.)

Before his death, Byck had sent tape recordings to celebrities in which he described what he intended to do, referring to his plan as "Operation Pandora's Box."

Our office had been asked to find tapes sent to Los Angeles.

Handing me a list, my supervisor instructed, "Go interview these people and see if they have any of Byck's tapes."

I quickly scanned the list and gasped. The first person on it was Steve Allen, consummate comedian, composer, pianist, and originator of *The Tonight Show*. He'd hosted the show before Jack Paar, Johnny Carson, or Jay Leno. It took me some time to find a phone number for his office and make an appointment. When I arrived, I was shown into his studio. He was sitting behind his desk dressed casually in a tan sweater and sporting his famous dark-rimmed glasses.

I introduced myself and showed him my credentials. "Thank you for taking the time to see me. We're investigating a man named Sam Byck, who you may have read about in the last couple of days. He tried to hijack a plane and fly it into the White House."

"Yes, I did hear about him. Isn't he dead?"

"You're correct, he's dead, but he mailed out a number of tape recordings to famous people outlining his plans. For some reason, the Secret Service believes you may be one of those people. Have you received any tape recordings from someone named Byck?"

"No, I haven't, but I'll tell my staff to keep an eye open for any packages from him. Do you know if he put a return address on them?" he asked.

"I don't think so. He mailed them in big white envelopes, if that's any help," I answered. "Well, again Mr. Allen, thank you again for your time. Here's my card. Call me if anything shows up in the next couple of days."

"I will. It was a pleasure meeting you."

I was star struck as I left the building. Climbing into my car, I looked at my list again. My next stop was Ray Charles. Flipping through my spiral-bound *Thomas Guide to Los Angeles and Orange County*, I found the address and plotted my way to his office, taking the Santa Monica Freeway to Washington Blvd. I finally found his famous studio and office building, RPM International Studio.

Blind since he was six years old, Ray Charles was sitting behind a piano, sporting his shades. I introduced myself, and he extended his hand, so I walked over to him and shook it. It seemed that he held it a very long time before letting go. My experience as a DC cop had sharpened my ability to identify addicts. He was only forty-three, but he looked like he was in his sixties. His speech seemed slow, and he was wearing an orange long-sleeved shirt, all the better to cover tracks. Charles had come to national attention in 1955 when he recorded "I Got a Woman," which combined gospel, jazz, and the blues. He laid the foundation for what would later become rock and roll and soul music. I knew I was shaking hands with greatness. In 2004, the movie *Ray* was released, in which Jamie Foxx played Ray Charles. Foxx won the 2005 Academy award for Best Actor.

I explained to Charles why I was there and asked if he'd received any of Byck's tapes. He politely answered my questions, saying he had not, but that would let me know if he did. I left my business card on his piano.

The following day, I had an appointment with Redd

Foxx's manager. Redd Foxx had been a comedian in the fifties and sixties, known for making raunchy party records. In the seventies, his star was rising as the head of a junkyard business in a popular NBC sitcom, *Sanford and Son*, which ran for six seasons. I never was able to meet him, but his manager had a package for me. Foxx *had* received one of Byck's tapes.

My last interview was with one of the writers for the TV series *Ironside*, which starred Raymond Burr. He played a former San Francisco chief of detectives forced to retire after a sniper's bullet. Working from his wheelchair, he continued to fight crime as a police consultant. The show ran for eight seasons and was nominated for two Golden Globe awards.

As I drove up to the gate of Universal Studios, I saw TV star Jack Webb standing there talking with one of the guards. When he saw me offer my credentials to the guard, he walked over to my car.

"Hi, could I take a look at your badge? I've never seen a Secret Service badge before," he said smiling.

He didn't even introduce himself, probably because he knew how recognizable he was as star of the police show *Dragnet*. I'd grown up watching him portray Sgt. Joe Friday on *Dragnet* every week. I was fascinated with police work even at age 6.

I reached out the car window and handed him my badge. He looked at it for a minute and handed it back to me.

"Good-looking badge," was all he said. It was enough. I'd briefly met my hero. Over the course of my career, I wrote great reports—"just the facts ma'am"—but only recently learned the saying came from *Dragnet*. Webb had tremendous respect for those in law enforcement. He wrote a book, *The Badge: True and Terrifying Crime Stories That Could Not be Presented on TV*, in which he discusses not only crimes like the Black Dahlia, but also what life was like for LAPD officers. Today, he is even more my hero.

I drove on into the Universal Studio visitor parking lot. It was a confusing place, but I finally found the building were Raymond Burr's writer was located. He told me Byck had not sent a tape to Burr, but he did offer me a job helping write scripts for the TV show *Ironside*. I didn't think the offer was a legitimate one, and I laughed it off. Today, I wonder if I had taken the writer up on his offer—if I had climbed through that open window of opportunity—how different my life might have been. But I didn't. On the other hand, if I had, I might have missed my opportunity to go to the Middle East.

Chapter 19:

July 1974: Souks and Sharks

The motorcade sped along the highway, turning their headlights on and off in the darkness. The night air was hot and dry, and the stars kissed the horizon.

"What are they doing turning their lights off?" I asked anyone who would listen. "We're going to crash into something!"

"Egyptians think they're saving their car battery," came an answer out of the darkness.

"Haven't they ever heard of an alternator?" I mumbled under my breath.

After a half hour of driving erratically, the motorcade pulled up in front of the Nile Hilton in Cairo. I scrambled out of the follow-up car and hurried to take my place beside Carol Simon, wife of William Simon, secretary of the US Treasury Department. Simon had been traveling back and forth to the Middle East to broker deals with OPEC in an attempt to lower gas prices. I had been sent back to DC to guard their house for several weeks. It seemed someone wanted me out of the LA office. As luck would have it, I'd gotten to know Mrs. Simon. When another Middle East trip came up, she decided to go with him. It was perfect timing because I was then the sole agent assigned to protect her on the trip.

William and Carol Simon

When we entered the hotel, there was a large crowd that we did not expect. As we wove our way through the throng of people, we quickly learned that they weren't there for us. There was a wedding, complete with music, dancing, and women ululating. I was wide-eyed, alert, and trying to take in everything—the sights, the sounds, the smells. It was surreal, as were the next thirteen days, during which we landed in nine countries and toured thirteen cities.

We arrived at the hotel at nine twenty at night, and because it was a free evening for the Simons, I had the night off. His detail would take care of protecting Mrs. Simon if they left their suite. I wandered around the hotel, peering through the glass into a modern gift shop. The night air flowed into the lobby and lured me outside. When I got to the door, I stopped dead in my tracks. Wide stone steps led down to the Nile River, and they were covered with a mass of huddled homeless men, women, and children cloaked in robes against the cold desert night. There was no room to walk among them, nor did I want to. I was alone and fearful. It was time to seek the safety of my room and get a good night's sleep.

The next morning, Mrs. Simon and her daughters, Mary Beth and Carol, came out of their suite exactly at ten as scheduled. She was tanned from swimming in their backyard pool in Maryland. Her brown hair was cut short and set off her brown eyes. She was dressed in a stylish lightweight dress with cap sleeves. Protocol required women's shoulders to be covered in the Middle East, even in the heat. Mrs. Eilts, wife of the American ambassador to Egypt, came out of the suite with them, and we made our way to a waiting air-conditioned limo. It was only a ten-minute drive to the Egyptian Museum, where a private tour had been arranged for our party. I rode in the limo with Mrs. Simon and her daughters.

An Egyptian security man drove, but I wasn't sure how much English he spoke. He knew where he was going, but we didn't. Worse, I couldn't communicate with him. It was a very uncomfortable situation for me. As I was the only Secret Service agent with Mrs. Simon for the whole trip, we were all on our own, in a sense. Mrs. Eilts was in the car behind us with the wife of one of the Egyptian ministers. Behind them were two more cars full of Egyptian security. I breathed a sigh of relief when we drove up to the door of the museum.

As we entered the museum, a pungent odor hit me, a mix of mustiness and death, emanating from relics that were thousands of years old. I knew little about Egyptian art, but I knew a mummy when I saw one. There was King Tutankhamun's golden tomb, and near it was Rameses II's mummified body lying in a glass case with one arm and hand slightly raised. His dark, leathery skin draped over his nose, cheekbones, and jaw line. I was amazed. His hair was even intact. Many consider him to be the greatest pharaoh of Egypt, but I considered him a miracle of ancient embalming practices.

We moved among the sarcophaguses slowly. I looked around at the security men in the room, in their white shirts and black pants. They all looked the same to me, and I realized that if a kidnapping or assassination attempt took place, for instance, I wouldn't know the good guys from the bad guys. I suppose if they were in the United States, they would think the same thing about male agents dressed in dark suits. My sense of duty to protect Mrs. Simon lay heavily on me. I wished I weren't the only agent with Mrs. Simon.

That afternoon, we joined Mr. Simon's party and motorcaded our way to the pyramids outside of Cairo. I pinched myself as I took in the Sphinx and the pyramids behind it. We climbed into the Great Pyramid, the oldest of the Seven Wonders of the World. We had to bend over to enter a small tunnel and start climbing up a gently sloping wooden walkway, carefully gaining a foothold with each step on cross boards. The large stone walls reached up on either side of us as we climbed deeper and deeper up into the pyramid. The air was a constant sixty-eight degrees Fahrenheit, a great reprieve from the desert heat. The pyramid had air shafts, which helped calm my fears. The stones hadn't moved in thousands of years, I told myself, so the odds they were going to move while we were inside were slim. We finally entered the main room, where an empty granite coffer sat. Stark light bulbs lighted the way. As we peered into the room, suddenly it went dark! The guide, wanting us to "feel" how dark it was inside the pyramid, had turned them off. My companions gasped in the complete blackness, but no one moved. I was thankful that I didn't have claustrophobia. After a few moments, the guide turned the lights back on—much to my relief. We carefully made our way down the descending shaft and adjusted our eyes as we emerged into the bright sunlight.

Mr. Simon's motorcade took the rest of the group back to the hotel, and I was relieved for a short time and told to ride back with one of the communications men. We came upon a young Egyptian boy holding a rope tethering a camel. Finally, my chance to have my photo taken atop a dromedary. As we neared the camel, its appalling smell flowed over us on a weak desert breeze. Camels urinate on their legs, and the odor is compounded by manure. I hesitated, wondering how much of the smell would rub off on my clothing, which I had no time to wash. Before I knew it, though, I was astride the blanketed saddle and the boy was motioning me to lean back. Suddenly, the camel rose up to his full height in one jerky movement. I quickly posed for a photo.

On a dromedary at the Great Pyramid in Egypt.

"OK, I'm done. Get me off this thing," I demanded. Not that it helped much—of course, the boy didn't speak English. He motioned again for me to lean back and gave the rope a slight downward jerk. The camel slowly dropped to its knees, and I unseated myself, hoping that the smell hadn't permeated my slacks.

Back at the hotel, I checked in with the detail leader in the command post.

"You can take the rest of the evening off, Sue Ann. They're all going to a dinner at the Sheraton at nine, hosted by First Deputy Prime Minister Hegazi. Mrs. Simon is going with him. We've got an early morning departure by train at eight, heading to Alexandria for the day. Mrs. Simon will be doing some sightseeing on her own and then join her husband at the yacht club for lunch. Then we're flying back to Cairo in the afternoon. Be here at seven."

I couldn't wait to get to my room and shower off the camel smell. My pants didn't reek too badly, so I draped them over a chair to air and then put on a clean outfit. I heard Middle Eastern music coming from the terrace off the lobby. Walking out into the cool desert air, I saw a vacant table, sat down, and ordered a glass of wine. A flurry of movement caught my eye, and when I turned, I saw three stunning Egyptian women belly dancing. Zills were tied to their middle fingers and thumbs. They clacked ancient rhythms, undulated their hips, and rippled their stomach muscles to the music. It was so fascinating to watch, I decided right then to take lessons in the future.

"They are amazing aren't they?" asked a heavily accented masculine voice beside me.

I looked up into the face of an Egyptian god—short black curly hair, wide-set dark eyes, perfect teeth and smile, a small goatee, and olive complexion. He was perfectly dressed in a white starched shirt with an open collar. "Yes, they are," I managed to say.

"May I sit down, or are you expecting someone?"

"I'm not expecting anyone. Yes, please have a seat."

Alarms were going off in my brain as the conversation proceeded. Was he a spy, and assassin, a kidnapper, or a gigolo? We watched the dancers for another half hour and talked. When he asked what I was doing in Cairo, I told him that I was a Secret Service agent and with an American delegation. His eyebrows raised and he seemed mildly surprised. After the dancers finished dancing, I decided it was time to hit the sack. He walked me to the elevator and said a charming good-bye, then shook my hand.

I got on alone and punched the elevator button to a floor that was one level below mine. When the door opened, I walked to the stairwell, taking the stairs two at a time to my floor. Safely in my room, I was still intensely curious. Whoever he really was, apparently I was not his type, or he'd decided I didn't have any secrets to reveal. Oh well.

The next morning, we boarded the train and rode north to Alexandria. Thankfully, we were in first class— with air conditioning. As I looked out the window of the swaying train, I saw a lone nomad leading his camel into the vast emptiness of the desert. It was like a scene from a movie. His robes were blowing and he had a scarf wrapped over his mouth and nose against the sand. *What a harsh life*, I thought. Where was he going and how long would it take him to get there?

The train eased into Sidi Gaber Station, and we motored to the Palestine Hotel. After some refreshments, Secretary Simon left for a meeting with President Sadat. Mrs. Simon and her family toured the Montazah Palace Gardens, planted on over a hundred acres of palace grounds. Meeting back at the yacht club, we ate a leisurely lunch. We were served a pitiful mound of melting chocolate ice cream for dessert. It was cooling, but hardly tasted like cocoa. When I came down with painful Middle Eastern trots two days later, the ice cream got the blame. Besides not drinking the water, including ice cubes, on foreign travels, I don't eat ice cream in countries with poor refrigeration.

Late that afternoon, we flew back to Cairo in two Russian Ilyushin prop airplanes. It was dusk as we arrived back at the Hilton. Learning that she had one and half hours free, Mrs. Simon headed for the hotel beauty parlor to get her hair done before an eight thirty private dinner with the American ambassador's wife and several embassy women. I sat beside her in a salon chair and watched her lean back to have her head massaged by the beautician washing her hair. I was so tired and it looked so wonderfully relaxing, but no matter how much I willed those fingers to be on my scalp, it didn't happen. There was no time for me.

The next day we flew to Tel Aviv for a brief stop in Israel. We managed to achieve a lot of sightseeing in a day and a half. We toured the Israel Museum , which houses the Dead Sea Scrolls, the Garden of Gethsemane, the Wailing Wall, Bethlehem, and the Dome of the Rock. For once, I didn't stick out like a sore thumb as the only female agent, because both men and woman are required to serve in the Israeli army. In a room full of US and Israeli agents, I made the mistake, however, of questioning how I could tell a Jewish Israeli from a Muslim Palestinian.

An Israeli security guy winked at me, looked down at his crotch, and said, "If you really want to know, there is an easy way to tell and I can show you." The room erupted in laughter. This time I had to laugh, too.

I held up both hands. "No, that's OK. I get the picture."

On the Via Dolorosa, a narrow, crowded street that winds through Jerusalem's old city, we visited the nine stations of the cross. The Simons were devout Catholics, and Mrs. Simon wanted her children to see them. This was the street that Jesus had supposedly walked, carrying the cross. I have since learned that there are several different routes through Jerusalem Jesus may have taken, but that he *may* have traveled this ancient stone street made our visit there a holy experience that I will never forget.

Next stop: Jeddah, Saudi Arabia. Our plane landed at six in the evening, but it was still scorching. As our plane pulled up to the gate, the women were told to stay on the plane, allowing the men to deplane first. Mr. Simon and his official party exited the plane and were met by his Saudi hosts. They proceeded to a VIP lounge and were served Arabic coffee. Finally, we were allowed off the plane, down the rear ramp, and escorted to our cars. The separation of men and women was strict in Saudi Arabia, and still is. I was appalled, but I dutifully sat with the other women in the air-conditioned cars and waited for the men.

The official motorcade to the US Embassy compound included eleven cars and one bus for the press. There were motorcycles, a lead car, and then the limousine with Secretary Simon, foreign ministers, and one Secret Service agent.

Next came two follow-up cars: one with four Secret Service agents, one with Saudi security. Then Mrs. Simon's car with the US ambassador's wife, Mrs. Akins, and me. The next car held the Simon children, and then another Saudi security car.

That night, I stood post outside the front door at a private home where the Simons were attending a dinner party. It was at least eleven before I headed to my room at the Kandara Palace Hotel. It had been a long day, but I feared the next one would be the killer.

We left the embassy at seven thirty the next morning and drove to the port, where the embassy yacht floated quietly in the still Red Sea. I stepped aboard, followed by Mrs. Simon, her daughters, her son, and several Saudi soldiers. After cruising for a half hour or so out to sea, the captain cut the engines. The Simons wanted to go snorkeling. I had my bathing suit on under a full-length robe, but I was embarrassed to take it off in front of the staring soldiers. This was a country where women were covered from head to toe and couldn't even let their shoulders show.

My orders were always to "stay close to Mrs. Simon," so I did, but I had limited experience with snorkeling. No one even gave me a shark bang stick, not that I would have known how to use it. Maybe I was just supposed to be the shark bait. Pushing that thought aside, I gathered up my courage and dove in. Floating in the warm, clear water and trying to keep up with Mrs. Simon, I concentrated on breathing normally. The colorful coral in the deep water was beautiful, and there were times I could not see the bottom, but that didn't bother me too much. What bothered me was what *could* be in the water. Finally, Mrs. Simon was finished snorkeling. The captain revved up the engine, and we headed back to the port.

With a Saudi on the American Embassy yacht in the Red Sea.

We arrived back at the embassy in time for lunch and an afternoon departure for the airport. I tried to comb my salt-encrusted hair as the motorcade wound its way through the city. Settling back in my seat on the plane, we lifted off for Taif, Saudi Arabia, to the summer home of the Minister of Oil and Mineral Resources, Sheik Yamani. Once in the air, I peered out the window at a vista of sand as far as the eye could see. Even if we survived a plane crash here, we wouldn't survive in the vastness of that inhospitable desert. I looked forward to landing in Taif, the lush, green summer capital of Saudi Arabia. At fifty-six hundred feet, the coolness there lured people from the dry desert lowlands to the mountains for months at a time.

Arriving at Hawiyah Airport, Mr. Simon was again met by royal protocol officials. We women again stayed on the plane until the men deplaned. It was all about protocol. The motorcade consisted of ten cars this time, followed by a luggage truck. Communications by telephone were nonexistent. The technical operations men operated a single-side band radio, which was the only communications link between us and the outside world. If anyone wanted to reach the embassy in Jeddah, they had to relay messages by radio to a US Military Training Mission compound command post. I was handed a radio at the airport for the ride to Sheik Yamani's summer home, so I had communications within in the motorcade.

The desert had turned from rolling sand to rocky terrain with a few sparse trees. Sheik Yamani's home rose out of it like a house built of Legos. At one end of the three-story rectangular house, a square addition jutted out toward the driveway. The stone house was set into a sheer rock cliff behind it. That cliff was an important security feature. A Saudi security man pointed out to me that there were men sitting in the rocks high up on the cliff. They blended in so well, it took me a little bit to find them. They sat there all night keeping vigil with their guns across their laps. We had been advised as agents to not show our weapons. They apparently weren't under the same orders.

At Sheik Yamani's summer home in Saudi Arabia.

I was given a room in the guest quarters, fortunately with a bathroom nearby. The Middle Eastern trots had hit me hard, and I found myself nearly doubled over with stomach cramps and diarrhea. Someone came by with a little white Lomotil tablet—that helped.

Dancing men at Sheik Yamani's dinner party.

I wandered around the compound and found a walled pit where young men were turning eight lambs skewered on long poles beneath a tent. A bed of coals smoldered under every two lambs. I couldn't imagine what the temperature was in that pit; it was in the nineties where I was standing. That evening, Sheik Yamani gave a large party complete with dancing men, jumping and whirling in their skirts—but not a belly dancer in sight.

Sheik Yamani's dinner party.

Dinner was laid out on long Persian carpets with pillows for the guests to sit on. I managed to get down a piece of bread with honey and some lamb. I didn't know what any of the other food was anyway.

The next morning, Mrs. Simon and the female dignitaries rode back to Taif for an extraordinary shopping experience in a Bedouin souk, an open-air market. The streets and alleyways were crowded. I was uneasy. We stood out as Americans—and as American women. Aromas enveloped us, some familiar and some unknowable. Large round woven baskets filled with spices and seeds lay on Persian carpets in front of vendors' stalls. I could identify red and black peppers; varying shades of green cardamom pods; light-brown cumin; red saffron; cloves; orange curry; and ginger. Many more spices, vegetables, and meats were displayed under the shade of canvas tents. Of course, there was also the Bedouin gold jewelry and tightly woven carpets. Mrs. Simon purchased little. When she did want to buy something, she borrowed money from me, as she never had time to exchange any of her own. That made for an interesting math problem when we headed home and she wanted to know what she owed me. She'd borrowed money in at least four different currencies. That day, however, we mostly looked and walked, sometimes pushing through the crowd, finally circling our way back to the waiting cars.

Mr. Simon met with King Faisal while we were shopping. He then had a private luncheon at the Khaldia Palace. The women were also given a private informal luncheon at the guest palace. After lunch, we headed to the airport. Wheels up for our last Middle East stop—Kuwait.

It was 130 degrees when we got off the airplane. We walked quickly down a red carpet on the tarmac, into the air-conditioned airport, into an air-conditioned car, and into an air-conditioned hotel. I don't know how anyone survived outside under the blast furnace of the desert sun.

Communications were tough in Kuwait at the time. I tried to call my brother, Jim, who was working in Shiraz, Iran, as a technical writer for Martin Marietta. He lived only about 275 miles from me, but I couldn't reach him. Even hearing the front desk from my hotel room on the phone was hard.

After a year in Iran, my brother came home. He'd gotten out just ahead of the country's slide into revolution and takeover by the Islamist Ayatollah Khomeini. He told me a story about meeting former vice president Spiro Agnew at a hotel in Shiraz. Agnew had already been forced to resign in October 1973 as vice president, amid accusations of extortion, bribery, and income-tax violations during his tenure as Maryland governor. While lounging by the hotel pool one day, Agnew lay down next to him.

Taking the initiative, my brother said, "Hi, my name's Jim Baker. Kinda hot out here today. I was just ready to get another Coke. Do you want one?"

"Thanks, I'm good. My name is Spiro. I hope you don't mind if I join you."

"No, of course not. It's always great to talk to another American." As the conversation continued, Jim mentioned that he had a sister who was a Secret Service agent. Agnew said, "Then your sister must be Sue Ann Baker." I was shocked to hear the story. Agnew knew Holly Hufschmidt, one of the other first five, because she'd protected his daughter. I'd never met him, but he knew who I was. That happened a lot when you're one of a handful of women in a sea of men.

Since I couldn't get a phone call though to Iran, I went back to my room and dressed for a formal dinner I had to accompany Mrs. Simon to that evening. There were about thirty women, sitting at tables in a big square formation. I was seated next to a woman from the State Department, which was a good thing because the silverware confused me, and State Department employees were legendary for their excellent etiquette. I watched her reach for a fork and followed her lead. After an appetizer and then soup, a delicious piece of white fish was placed on my plate. It was so good that when the waitress came to offer me more fish, I said yes.

The State Department woman leaned toward me and quietly said, "Sue Ann, you should probably know that this is only the third course, and not the main course. This is a sixteen-course dinner. But then, maybe you're really hungry."

I looked at her wide-eyed, happily chewing my second piece of fish. "Are you kidding me? Who can eat that much food?"

"No, I'm not kidding. Enjoy," she replied smiling.

That October, Mrs. Simon mailed me a photo of her walking out of that dinner with me behind her. The card read, *Dear Sue Ann, Thought you might like to have this as a remembrance of the night I ate sixteen courses before your very eyes!!* I guess I wasn't the only one impressed with the dinner.

Mrs. Simon, center, with me behind her, leaving the 16-course dinner.

On our way back to the United States, we made several stops. The first was Rome, where we motorcaded to the pope's summer palace in Gandolfo. We lunched there and drove back to the airport in time to fly to Hamburg for the night. The next day, we arrived in London. I finally had some time off in the early afternoon, but I never left the hotel room. Still feeling the effects of the ice cream in Egypt, I didn't venture too far from a bathroom. Piccadilly Circus would have to wait for another visit.

Our very last stop was a brief layover in Bermuda. I adored the warm, sandy beaches. The Simons went swimming, another agent and I dressed in bathing suits ready to dive in with them. Bill Simon seemed relaxed at last after the demanding schedule of his Middle East trip. The beach was crowded with bathers, some top-less.

"Hey, Sue Ann," he yelled above the surf. "Why don't you take your top off so you blend in more with the other gals on the beach?"

"Nice try, sir, but I think I'll keep it on today." It was the first time I'd experienced his sense of humor. Mrs. Simon laughed and dove into the surf. I was right behind her.

Chapter 20:

October 1974: Wonder Woman Moves On: Leaving the Secret Service to Become a Private Investigator in LA

It was a difficult decision to leave the Secret Service and the security of a government job. My parents were nervous about my future. The Watergate scandal, beginning with the burglary of the Democratic National Committee's office in the Watergate Hotel, had festered for two years. The tape recordings in the Oval Office proved that Nixon had knowledge of the burglary and tried to cover it up. His choice: resignation or impeachment. He chose resignation on August 8, 1974. I had passed him in the White House ten days before. His unsmiling face was covered in pancake makeup. It was pale and drawn, exposing the tremendous stress he was under. I knew then that it wouldn't be long before his presidency would come to an end.

The US was in a recession, and the stock market had lost over 45% of its value in the previous two years. I hadn't lived through a depression like my parents, so I was oblivious to the potential hardships. I never felt the effects of it with my government job and steady income. I must have been aware of what was happening, but I was excited and optimistic about my transition into the civilian world. I thanked my wise parents for their concern, and tendered my resignation. In the end, being my own boss as a private investigator in Los Angeles appealed to me more than staying the course. I wanted to control not only my life, but also my time and my income. Deep down, I've always had an entrepreneurial spirit, a spirit that didn't mesh well with the militaristic structure and bureaucracy of federal law enforcement.

I resigned effective October 11, 1974.

My resignation stated, "I feel that I have undergone personal growth and change, in terms of future aspirations and goals, in such a way as to conflict with my position as a Special Agent. I realize that the US Secret Service is a way of life, encompassing a lifestyle and dedication I can no longer give. For these reasons, in the best interest of the US Secret Service and myself, I feel compelled to resign." I was a government service grade nine, step one, and left a job paying $12,167 a year—$58,425 a year in 2014 dollars.

By the time I turned in my gun and badge, the Secret Service was hiring more female agents and I decided that my duty was done. Of the five original female agents, only three remained at that point. Kathy Clark, who had protected the Queen of Spain and Caroline Kennedy, was the first to make her decision to leave because she was getting married. The Secret Service wouldn't transfer her anywhere near her husband-to-be, or she would have stayed. She had been transferred to LA, and we were roommates at the time. I know how agonizing it was for her to make a decision between the two loves of her life. Phyllis Shantz, transferred to New York, and was eventually assigned to the permanent vice presidential detail, protecting Walter Mondale. She often worked undercover during counterfeit investigations in NYC and LA. During the 1972 campaign, they had her running all over the country from one protection detail to another undercover assignment. She didn't come home for seven months. Her favorite protectee was Golda Meir, whom she got to know very well and loved. After ten years of service, Phyllis transferred as an agent to the ATF and retired from them in 1998. Holly Hufschmidt worked for six years. During that time, she protected several foreign dignitaries: the prime minister of Israel; the shah of Iran's wife; German chancellor Willy Brandt's wife; and Golda Meir. She said that while on the presidential campaign trail, protecting Jimmy Carter in Georgia, the male detail agents seemed to have a hard time getting to work on time. She was told to call each of them in the morning and wake them up. To her credit, she refused. Laurie Anderson was the only one of us to retire from the Secret Service. She continued her legacy as a first woman when she was assigned to the Office of Government Liaison and Public Affairs, to the Fraud and Forgery Division, INTERPOL and then to the Office of Inspection. She eventually also became the first woman agent supervisor in the Secret Service Intelligence Division and Special Investigation and Security Division. She truly was a testament to strength and endurance.

Those four women and I had cracked the glass ceiling, but it hadn't immediately shattered. The Service has continued to hire women, but we still only account for 10% of the agents. It isn't enough. According to Linda Tarr-Whelan in her book *Women Lead the Way*, an organization needs at least 30% women in a leadership group, at which point different decisions are made: "Why 30%? This has proved to be the critical mass in any group of decision makers, the tipping point at which women's voices resonate fully to add the affirmative difference of our experiences and values."

The personal growth I experienced and the confidence I gained as a member of the Secret Service can't be measured. Not only did I travel the world in my time with the organization, I made history and also witnessed history being made.

On the Secret Service's website, www.secretservice. gov, there is a list of conditions of employment. They include:

- Working long hours in undesirable conditions on short notice.

- Travel away from home for periods up to 30 days, and sometimes longer.

- Carrying a firearm while performing duties, and maintaining firearms proficiency.
- Carrying out assignments in the areas of both protection and investigations.
- Relocating to duty stations throughout the US and abroad as organizational needs dictate.
- Agents may be requested to work undercover assignments.

I can attest to all of these conditions. Been there, done that.

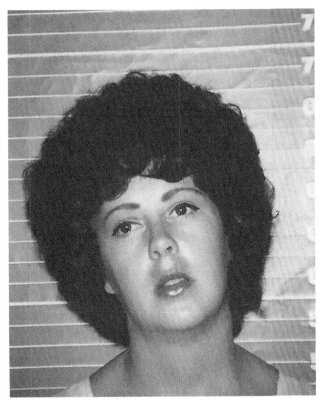

Working undercover.

I'm proud of the four years I spent working for the agency and serving my country. The Secret Service is a fantastic organization whose dedicated employees often make unimaginable sacrifices. Only those who have dedicated their lives to it will truly understand what it takes, and the toll it can take, to be part of this family. Any sacrifices I made helped me gain more confidence and assertiveness. I was moving up the scale of being an alpha woman.

With my resignation, I knew that I would again be playing it by ear on my own, but this time the tune would be familiar, and I could even pick the instrument.

Epilogue

I was still getting dressed when the phone rang.

"Hello, is Sue Ann Baker there?"
"Yes, this is she."
"Hi, this is Eleanor McGovern."
"Yeah, right! Who is this really?"

And then I heard laughter—a high-pitched, frail laugh from an elderly woman. "No, this really is Eleanor McGovern. I just called to wish you a happy sixtieth birthday."

"Oh my gosh," I stammered. "Thank you. How are you? How did you know it was my birthday?" I had all kinds of questions for her.

"A fellow from George's library called and said that someone, a good friend of yours, had called him asking to get in touch with me. He passed the message along. I just didn't know whether to call you at four p.m. your time or my time, so I decided on my time." We chatted for a good fifteen minutes. I was so glad she'd called two hours before my party started. I wouldn't have been able to hear her weak voice if my house had been full of people.

"Do you remember the time you and Mary Hoyt stood on your head in the hotel suite?" I asked.

"No, I never did that, or at least, I don't remember doing it."

This time I laughed, because I remembered it so

well. It was one of the rare light-hearted moments we shared during a brutal presidential campaign. "Well, you did, but you cheated and put your feet against the wall."

We caught up. I shared that my husband of twenty-five years had died in 2001, and she told me about her daughter Teresa's death after battling alcoholism for years. Eleanor never mentioned that she, herself, had heart problems. As the conversation wound down, we both agreed to keep in touch. I sent her a thank-you letter and small gift, but never heard back from her. Six months later, I read that she'd died of heart failure at eighty-five. Impossible. It didn't seem that long ago we were zigzagging across the country on the campaign trail. The last time I'd seen her, she was a young, vibrant woman, defining new roles for campaigning wives, as she took to the road by herself. Of course, I hadn't aged in my mind, either.

Recipes

Eleanor McGovern's Pork and Apple Pie
Given to Agent Denise Ferrenz by Mrs. McGovern

1 ½ lb. boneless pork diced
¾ cup chopped onion
1 ½ tsp rubbed sage
2 tsp salt
¼ tsp pepper
¼ cup cracker meal
2 tart cooking apples thinly sliced
2 tbls lemon juice
2 tbls flour

Preheat oven to 325. Combine pork, onion, sage, salt, pepper, meal and toss. In separate bowl mix apple, lemon juice, and flour. Layer apples and pork. Cover with foil. Bake 1 ½–2 hours. 10 min. before serving, make topping, brush with butter. Run under broiler 5–7 min. Let stand 5 min.

Makes 4 servings.

Topping: ½ package 5 5/8 oz instant mashed potatoes
1 tsp salt
2 tbls butter
½ cup milk
1 tbls butter melted.

Vodka Pasta
Prepared for President Nixon's 75th Birthday

1 lb. pasta (farfalle, penne rigate, rigatoni, etc.)
3 Tbsp olive oil
1/3 cup butter
1 medium onion, diced
1 cup red pepper, diced
1/3 cup vodka
2 cups Roma tomatoes, seeded and chopped, or 1 12-oz can crushed tomatoes
1 pt. heavy whipping cream
1/2 tsp red pepper flakes (optional)
3/4 cup grated Parmesan or Pecorino cheese
2 Tbsp salt for pasta water

Put a large pot (8-10 qt.) on stove to boil. In another pan, sauté onion and peppers in olive oil and butter for 8–10 min. Stir in red pepper flakes. Add the vodka and boil for 6 min. before adding chopped tomatoes. Cook over med. heat until the liquid evaporates and the sauce begins to bind.

Add the cream and heat to a boil, cooking until the sauce thickens and coats the back of a wooden spoon. When the water is boiling, add salt—when water returns to a rapid boil, add the pasta. Cook pasta for 8 min. Take out 1 cup of pasta water (set aside), drain pasta, and return it to pot on the stove.

Add 3/4 of the sauce, 1/2 of the water, and boil until pasta begins to glisten (6-8 min.). Add more sauce, if needed. Turn off heat and add grated cheese, 1/4 cup at a time, stirring until blended. Serve with additional grated cheese and red pepper flakes.

Compliments of the US Secret Service Employee Recreation Association Cookbook

.

Sue Ann Baker

In 1971, with her back to the flashing cameras, Sue Ann Baker raised her hand to be sworn in as a Secret Service agent. During the 1972 presidential campaign, she crisscrossed the county protecting presidential hopeful Shirley Chisholm and Senator McGovern's wife, Eleanor, and later joined a diplomatic mission on a thirteen-day, ten-country trip to the Middle East. In 1974, Sue Ann left the Service to become a private eye, first in Los Angeles and then St. Thomas, US Virgin Islands, while living on a forty-foot sailboat and working cases for Lloyd's of London. She recently retired after twenty-one years as a financial planner for Waddell & Reed, and lives in Roseburg, Oregon. To invite Sue Ann to speak, please visit her website: www.sueannbaker.com.

Made in the USA
Middletown, DE
01 September 2024

60171384R00145